the

the guide to art exhibitions 2002

Great Britain and Ireland

With an introduction by David Cohen

Lund Humphries

First published in 2001 by
Lund Humphries
Gower House
Croft Road
Aldershot
Hampshire GU11 3HR

and

131 Main Street
Burlington
VT 05401 USA

www.lundhumphries.com

Lund Humphries is part of Ashgate Publishing

Copyright © 2001 Lund Humphries

British Library Cataloguing-in-Publication Data
A catalogue record for this book is available from the British Library

All rights reserved. No part of this publication may be reproduced, stored in a retrieval system or transmitted in any form or by any means, electrical, mechanical or otherwise, without first seeking the permission of the publishers.

ISBN 0 85331 838 7

Compiled by Kate Ferrie
Edited by Ian Heath
Designed by Mick Keates
Typeset in Helvetica by Tom Knott

Printed in Belgium by Snoeck-Ducaju & Zoon

Introduction

The Guide to Art Exhibitions 2002

A few years ago the Royal Academy of Arts mounted an exhibition I'll never forget. *The Art Treasures of England: The Regional Collections* literally dropped a new national museum into the city, albeit for a few months. The walls were densely hung, in emulation of the eminently Victorian institutions from which many of the exhibits were culled, and the quality was startling and rich. To say 'I had no idea' was admitting to metropocentrism, but even a Londoner (as I then was) who took pride in getting himself to Glasgow and Edinburgh and Liverpool and Cardiff and Dublin when the excuse presented itself felt a little humbled not to have known about some of those treasures. With the aid of the venerable Lund Humphries *Guide*, which of course extends throughout the sceptered isle and the emerald one, too, opportunities for art-hunting abound.

Permanent collections are just the sitting targets. The *Guide* gives the inside scoop on moving ones too. I have jotted down a list of 'unmissables' in the coming year, but I could easily spend the next twelve months on the road, and I don't even live in London these days (a new New Yorker, I'm just getting used to the idea of London as destination rather than epicentre).

I'd like to get myself to Strathclyde to see the Terry Setch retrospective at the Collins Gallery. Setch is an original heir of the romantic sublime tradition, a reinventor of the landscape genre. I have enjoyed isolated shows of his, but would be most curious to see how his career measures up when seen in the round.

Then I notice that Nigel Henderson is getting his due. He was a seminal force in the 1950s London avantgarde. Among the young spirits at the ICA – Paolozzi, Turnbull and Hamilton fared better in terms of career development – he was the true polymath, a bridger of art and science at a fascinating cultural moment. His gang will feature, no doubt, in the Barbican's survey of the London art scene in the 1950s. Meanwhile, Richard Hamilton's *Ulysses* etchings get an airing in Bloom's city, at the Irish Museum of Modern Art, where an international line up includes Thomas Ruff and Sol LeWitt.

Thanks to the enterprise and tenacity of the Henry Moore Foundation, I often found myself on the 9.10 from Kings Cross to do the 'golden triangle' of the Henry Moore Studio at Dean Clough, Halifax, the Yorkshire Sculpture Park, and the Henry Moore Institute in Leeds – to be back in time for tea. It was always a pleasure on those trips to catch up with Robert Hopper, a man who played a vital role in the foundation of all three institutions which really helped make Yorkshire a vital place for sculpture. Sadly, Robert died last year, but the venues he was associated with go from strength to strength. I see the Institute, which he directed, has a show of English polychromy. In their stark, well-lit, modernist galleries it should look stunning and may well be an eye-opener too. The YSP, I know, has exciting things planned, so check their website.

Watch out you don't get confused in Liverpool. I had to read twice: the Tate there has a show of the abjectionist performance artist from California, Paul McCarthy, while the Walker is showing the paintings of native rock legend Paul McCartney. Very different artists. One is an ex-Beatle, the other – on a restrained day - eats beetles for breakfast.

For more refined pleasures one could do well to stay in the vicinity of Somerset House. The Courtauld is offering the rich and penetrating show we enjoyed here in New York at the Metropolitan Museum, of Leon Kossoff's transcriptions of Poussin, while in the Hermitage Rooms, there is a display of French paintings from Poussin to Picasso. What an odd art world it is, in these days of globalisation, that to view St Petersburg's treasures you can be beside the Thames or in a casino in Las Vegas. Also in cosmopolitan London the Estorick Collection, dedicated to the Italian avantgarde, has a Carlo Carrà exhibit one should be sorry to miss.

The Museum of Modern Art in Oxford has a long-standing reputation for introducing British audiences to major modern Americans, and the tradition seems to continue with a show of the veteran, super-cool LA pop/conceptual artist Ed Ruscha. Forgive me if I pick out so many Americans from the menu. Even New Yorkers can get provincial.

David Cohen

David Cohen is an art historian, critic, lecturer and curator. He is editor of the on-line journal, artcritical.com, and Gallery Director at the New York Studio School.

Whilst all information given in the *Guide to Art Exhibitions* is correct at the time of going to press, we strongly advise that details of exhibitions are confirmed with the individual galleries before planning a visit, as the information provided to us is subject to change.

Key to Symbols
■ Exhibition (not touring)
➤ Touring exhibition
➤ *The sequence of the tour venues*
* Publication planned to accompany the exhibition

NTE: National Touring Exhibition

Aberdeen

Aberdeen Arts Centre, 33 King Street, Aberdeen,
Grampian, AB24 5AA
tel (01224) 635208 *fax* (01224) 626390
The Centre has a 350-seat theatre and a small gallery. Exhibitions of art, craft and photography change monthly and mainly celebrate the work of local artists. Opening times are 10:00–4:00 Monday–Saturday, and evenings for performances. Please phone for full details of current exhibitions.

Aberdeen Art Gallery, Schoolhill, Aberdeen, Grampian, AB10 1FQ
tel (01224) 523700 *fax* (01224) 523690
website www.aberdeencity.gov.uk *e-mail* info@aagm.co.uk
The gallery houses an important collection ranging from 18th-century portraits by Raeburn, Hogarth and Reynolds, to 20th-century works by Paul Nash, Ben Nicholson and Francis Bacon, and Impressionist works by Monet, Pisarro, Sisley and Bonnard. Other permanent displays include Scottish silver and other decorative arts. Please phone or consult the website for full details of current exhibitions.

Aberford

Lotherton Hall, Aberford, West Yorkshire, LS25 3EB
tel (0113) 281 3259 *fax* (0113) 281 2100
website www.leeds.gov.uk
An Edwardian country house, formerly home of the Gascoigne family, containing fine collections of paintings, furniture, sculpture, metalwork, ceramics and jewellery, with special displays of fashion and Oriental art.

- ■ Masterpieces of Contemporary Craft from the Permanent Collection of the Crafts Council — late Spring – Summer 02

Aberford (Lotherton Hall) > Aldershot

➤ Contemporary Broad-Bladed 21 June – 20 Aug 02
Silver Servers*
➤ *Aberford* ➤ *Edinburgh* ➤ *Aberdeen* ➤ *Leeds* ➤ *Nottingham*

Aberystwyth
Ceramic Gallery Arts Centre, School of Art, University College
of Wales, Aberystwyth, Buarth Mawr, Dyfed, SY23 1NG
tel (01970) 622460 *fax* (01970) 622461
website www.aber.ac.uk. *e-mail* mov@aber.ac.uk
The gallery houses contemporary British, European, American and
Japanese studio pottery, 18th- and 19th-century Welsh and English
slipware and porcelain, art pottery and Oriental ceramics, as well as
an important collection of early 20th-century British pioneer studio
pottery. Please phone or consult the website for full details of
current exhibitions.

School of Art Gallery & Museum, The University of Wales,
Aberystwyth, Buarth Mawr, SY23 1NG
tel (01970) 622460 *fax* (01970) 622461
website www.aber.ac.uk/museum *e-mail* neh@aber.ac.uk
The gallery holds extensive collections of fine and decorative art,
European prints from the 15th century to the present, drawings,
watercolours, photographs, wood engravings, pottery and slipware.
It also houses the George Powell of Nanteos collection of pictures,
bronzes and *objets d'art*. Please phone or consult the website for full
details of current exhibitions.

Aldershot
West End Centre Gallery, Queens Road, Aldershot,
Hampshire, GU11 3JD
tel (01252) 408040 *fax* (01252) 408041

Aldershot (West End Centre) > Appledore

An arts centre with a programme ranging from two- and three-dimensional exhibitions to theatre, comedy, film, music and classes. Please phone for full details of current exhibitions.

Alston

Gossipgate Gallery, The Butts, Alston, Cumbria, CA9 3JU
tel (01434) 381806 *fax* (01434) 381908
The permanent collection comprises works on paper, sculpture, ceramics, jewellery, glass and textiles by many contemporary artists.

Ambleside

Dexterity, Kelsick Road, Ambleside, Cumbria, LA22 0BZ
tel (015394) 34045
e-mail dext@btinternet.com
The gallery's collection includes collographs, lithographs, etchings, mixed media, screenprints, ceramics and glass, as well as oils and watercolours, by numerous contemporary artists. Please phone for full details of current exhibitions.

Grizedale Arts, Grizedale Society, Ambleside, Cumbria, LA22 0QJ
tel (01229) 860291 *fax* (01229) 860050
website www.grizedale.org *e-mail* info@grizedale.org
Please phone or consult the website for full details of current exhibitions.

Appledore

Gallerie Marin, 31 Market Street, Appledore, North Devon, EX39 1PP
tel (01237) 473679/474231 *fax* (01237) 421655
Contemporary paintings with an emphasis on marine art, including work by Mark Myers, David Brackman, Tim Thompson, Michael Lees, Jenny Morgan, Gordon Frickers, Vincent Neave, Robert

Blackwell, Richard Slater and Jonathon Sainsbury. Please phone for full details of current exhibitions.

Aylesbury
Bucks County Museum, Church Street, Aylesbury, Buckinghamshire, HP20 2QP
tel (01296) 331441 *fax* (01296) 334884
website www.buckscc.gov.uk/museum
e-mail museum@buckscc.gov.uk
Please phone or consult the website for full details of current exhibitions.

Ballymoney
Stables Gallery, Ballywindland House, Ballywindelland Road, Ballymoney, Co. Antrim, Northern Ireland, BT53 6QT
tel (02827) 665919
website www.stablesgallery.co.uk
e-mail stewart.moore@btinternet.com
The Stables Gallery's permanent collection comprises 20th-century and contemporary Irish art. Please phone or consult the website for full details of current exhibitions.

- ■ Spring Exhibition of Irish Art* 16 – 19 Mar 02
- ■ David Gordon Hughes: New Paintings* 4 – 8 May 02
- ■ Summer Exhibition of Irish Art* 6 – 31 July 02
- ■ Colin Davidson: New Paintings* 5 – 9 Oct 02
- ■ Christmas Exhibition of Irish Art* 30 Nov – 24 Dec 02

Banbury
Graphicus Touring, 36 Bloxham Road, Banbury, Oxfordshire, OX16 9JN
tel/fax (01295) 256110

website www.graphicustouring.com
e-mail leodefreitas@graphicustouring.com
Creator of touring exhibitions. Please phone for full details.

Bangor
Bangor Museum & Art Gallery, Fford Gwynedd, Bangor, Gwynedd, LL57 1DT
tel (01248) 353368
e-mail davidhuntington@gwynedd.gov.uk
Please phone for full details of current exhibitions.

Barnard Castle
The Bowes Museum, Barnard Castle, Co. Durham, DL12 8NP
tel (01833) 690606 *fax* (01833) 637163
website www.bowesmuseum.org.uk
e-mail info@bowesmuseum.org.uk
An outstanding collection of European fine and decorative art, including works by El Greco, Canaletto, Goya, Tiepolo and Boudin, and the most important collection of Spanish paintings in the UK. Displays include costume, toys, ceramics and musical instruments, and there is an annual programme of temporary exhibitions. Please phone or consult the website for details. Open 11:00–5:00 daily.

Barrow in Furness
Dock Museum, North Road, Barrow in Furness, Cumbria, LA14 2PW
tel (01229) 894444 *fax* (01229) 811361
Though the museum concentrates on the social and industrial history of Barrow and the surrounding area, it also houses a fine art collection including works by George Rowney. Please phone for full details.

Basingstoke

Willis Museum & Art Gallery, Old Town Hall, Market Place, Basingstoke, Hampshire, RG21 1QD
tel (01256) 465902
website www.hants.gov.uk/museums *e-mail* musmst@hants.gov.uk
Please phone or consult the website for full details of current exhibitions.

Bath

The American Museum, Claverton Manor, Bath, Avon, BA2 7BD
tel (01225) 460503 *fax* (01225) 480726
website www.americanmuseum.org *e-mail* amibbath@aol.com
A series of furnished rooms showing how Americans lived from the late 17th to mid-19th centuries. There are also galleries of decorative arts (pewter, silver and glass), Native American objects and American folk art.

- ■ The North American Indian   23 Mar – 3 Nov 02

Anthony Hepworth Fine Art Dealers, 1 Margaret's Buildings, Brock Street, Bath, Avon, BA1 2LP
tel (01225) 47480 *fax* (01225) 42917
Dealers specialising in 20th-century British and contemporary painting, sculpture and drawing, as well as African tribal art.

Beaux Arts, 12–13 York Street, Bath, BA1 1NG
tel (01225) 464850 *fax* (01225) 422256
e-mail beauxart@netcomuk.uk
The gallery specialises in the work of major 20th-century and young contemporary British painters and sculptors and leading modern ceramicists. Established artists include Michael Ayrton, Lynn Chadwick, Elisabeth Frink, John Piper and especially the St Ives

Bath (Beaux Arts)

group, including Terry Frost, Barbara Hepworth, Bryan Pearce and William Scott.

Holburne Museum of Art, Great Pulteney Street, Bath, Avon, BA2 4DB
tel (01225) 466669 *fax* (01225) 333121
website www.bath.ac.uk/holburne
e-mail holburne@bath.ac.uk
Fine and decorative art includes Old Masters, English and Continental silver, porcelain, glass, Renaissance bronzes and Italian maiolica. The Picture Gallery contains works by Stubbs, Turner, Guardi and others plus portraits of Bath society by Thomas Gainsborough. Open 10:00–5:00 Tuesday–Saturday, 2:30–5:30 Sunday, mid-February to mid-December. Guided tours by arrangement.

- A Pelican in the Wilderness: Hermits and Hermitages — Mar – May 02
- Pickpocketing the Rich: Portrait Painters in Bath 1720–1793 — June – Aug 02

Rostra Gallery, 5 George Street, Bath, Avon, BA1 2EH
tel (01225) 448121 *fax* (01225) 447421
website www.rostragallery.co.uk
e-mail info@rostragallery.co.uk
Dealers in contemporary modern art, including limited edition prints, original paintings, sculpture, ceramics, glass and jewellery.

Victoria Art Gallery, Bridge Street, Bath, Avon, BA2 4AT
tel (01225) 477233 *fax* (01225) 477231
website www.victoriagal.org.uk
e-mail victoria_enquiries@bathnes.gov.uk

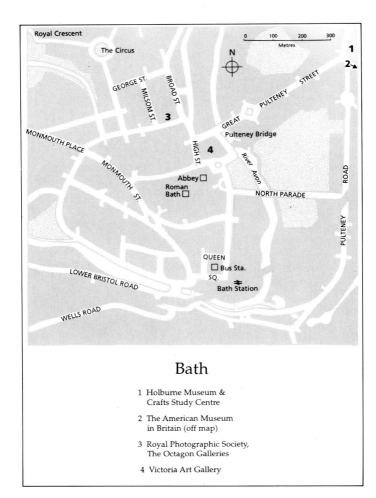

Bath (Victoria Art Gallery)

- ■ Nature from Wood: Guy Taplin, Howard Phipps, Colin See-Paynton, Chris Wormell — To 6 Jan 02
- ► Cartoons from the Permanent Collection — To 3 Feb 02
  - ➤ *Victoria Art Gallery, Bath* ➤ *Durham Art Gallery*
- ► The Snake in the Garden: Contemporary Approaches to Slipware* — 13 Jan – 10 Mar 02
  - ➤ *Collins Gallery, Glasgow* ➤ *Victoria Art Gallery, Bath* ➤ *Tullie House Museum & Art Gallery, Carlisle*
  - *Originated by Aberystwyth Arts Centre*
- ► Travelling Companions: Chardin and Freud* — 9 Feb – 7 Apr 02
  - *Originated by the National Gallery, London*
- ■ Nicola Hicks: Sculptures in Plaster and Straw plus Drawings* — 16 Mar – 16 June 02
- ■ Jane Joseph, Printmaker — 13 Apr – 9 June 02
- ■ Paul Sonnabend Paintings — 15 June – 4 Aug 02
- ► Mirror Mirror: Self-Portraits by Women Artists* — 22 June – 1 Aug 02
  - ➤ *National Portrait Gallery, London* ➤ *City Art Gallery, Leeds* ➤ *Victoria Art Gallery, Bath*
- ■ Bath Society of Artists 97th Annual Exhibition* — 10 Aug – 15 Sept 02
- ■ Innocence and Austerity: The Art of Ben Hartley (1933–96)* — 21 Sept – 24 Nov 02
- ■ John Eaves: New Watercolours and Collages — 21 Sept – 24 Nov 02
- ■ Peter Brown: New Paintings and Drawings of Bath — 30 Nov 02 – 26 Jan 03
- ■ Bathing in Bath — 30 Nov 02 – 2 Mar 03

Bedford

Bromham Mill & Gallery, Bedfordshire County Council, County Hall, Cauldwell Street, Bedford, MK42 9AP
tel (01234) 228330 *fax* (01234) 228531
website www.borneo.co.uk/bromham_mill
The Mill and Gallery hosts a regularly changing programme of contemporary arts and crafts exhibitions, including jewellery, ceramics, glass and more from the Fenny Lodge Gallery, as well as local artists and touring exhibitions. Please phone or consult website for full details.

Cecil Higgins Art Gallery, Castle Lane, Bedford, MK40 3RP
tel (01234) 211222 *fax* (01234) 327149
website www.cecilhigginsartgallery.org *e-mail* chag@bedford.gov.uk

- Watercolours from the Higgins Collection* To 7 Apr 02
- Enamelling for Quality: Enamels by Ernestine Mills 16 Apr – 14 July 02
- Lace from the Cecil Higgins Art Gallery July – Sept 02
- Tissot and his London Circle Oct 02 – Jan 03

Beer

Marine House at Beer, Fore Street, Beer, Devon, EX12 3EF
tel (01297) 625257
website www.marinehouse-at-beer.co.uk
e-mail info@marinehouse-at-beer.co.uk
Marine House at Beer hosts a wide and constantly changing range of paintings, ceramics, sculpture, glassware, jewellery and more, by new and established artists from both the West Country and further afield. Please phone or consult the website for full details of current exhibitions.

- Tina Morgan: New Works* Mar 02

■ Andrew Coates* 30 June – 13 July 02

Belfast

Bell Gallery, 13 Adelaide Park, Belfast, Northern Ireland, BT9 6FX
tel (02890) 662998
website www.bellgallery.com *e-mail* bellgallery@btinternet.com
Please phone or consult the website for full details of current exhibitions. Open 9:30–5:00 Monday–Thursday, 9:30–3:00 Friday.

- James Mackeown: Paintings Mar 02
- John Breakey: Paintings, Watercolours and Graphics Apr 02
- Belfast Festival Exhibition Nov 02
- Christmas Group Show: Paintings and Sculpture Dec 02

Eakin Gallery, 237 Lisburn Road, Belfast, Northern Ireland, BT9 7EN
tel/fax (02890) 668522
website www.eakingallery.co.uk
e-mail eakin@paintings.freeserve.co.uk
Please phone or consult the website for full details of current exhibitions.

- St Patrick's Day Exhibition of Irish Art* 17 – 24 Mar 02
- Modern Ulster* May 02
- Christmas Exhibition 24 Nov – Dec 02

Fenderesky Gallery, Crescent Arts Centre, 2–4 University Road, Belfast, Northern Ireland, BT7 1NH
tel (02890) 235245 *fax* (02890) 246748
The gallery holds a permanent collection which concentrates on contemporary Irish art, and organises about sixteen exhibitions each year. Please phone for full details of current exhibitions.

Belfast

Old Museum Arts Centre, 7 College Square, North Belfast, Northern Ireland, BT1 6AR
tel (01232) 235053 *fax* (01232) 322912
website www.oldmuseumartscentre.org
e-mail anna@oldmuseumartscentre.org
Please phone or consult the website for full details of current exhibitions.

■ Amanda McKittrick	To 19 Jan 02
■ Source Commission	24 Jan – 15 Feb 02
■ Jean Duncan	21 Feb – 16 Mar 02
■ Source Commission	21 Mar – 13 Apr 02
■ Belfast Print Workshop Group Show	18 Apr – 31 May 02

Ulster Museum, Botanic Gardens, Belfast, Northern Ireland, BT9 5AB
tel (02890) 383000 *fax* (02890) 383003
website ulstermuseum.org.uk
Open 10:00–5:00 Monday–Friday, 1:00–5:00 Saturday, 2:00–5:00 Sunday. There are facilities for disabled visitors. Admission is free, please phone or consult the website for full details of current exhibitions.

■ Fashion Now	To 6 Jan 02
■ Texaco Children's Art	To 20 Jan 02
■ Derek Hill 1916–2000	To 7 Apr 02
■ Glass and Ceramic Sculpture	To Spring 02
■ In the Firing Line: Contemporary Ceramics	To Spring 02
■ James Glen Wilson: Artist and Traveller	To Spring 02
■ The Saatchi Gift through the National Art Collections Fund	To Summer 02
■ Contemporary Irish Art	To Summer 02
■ Op and Kinetic Art	To Summer 02

- Works on Paper   To Aug 02
- Aspects of Asia   To Dec 02
- Matisse and Belfast   18 Jan – June 02
- Stanley Spencer   25 Jan – 7 Apr 02

Organised by Tate Britain, London

Berwick upon Tweed

The Paxton Trust, Paxton House, Berwick upon Tweed, Northumberland, TD15 1SZ
tel (01289) 386291 *fax* (01289) 386660
The Trust is home to a major collection of Chippendale and the largest picture gallery in any Scottish country house, now an outstation of the National Galleries of Scotland. Please phone for full details of current exhibitions.

Bewdley

Bewdley Museum, Load Street, Bewdley, Worcestershire, DY12 2AE
tel (01299) 403573 *fax* (01299) 404740
e-mail museum_wfde@online.rednet.co.uk
The museum is open between 29 March–31 October, from 11:00 a.m. to 5:00 p.m. until September and 11:00 a.m. to 4:00 p.m. in October. It focuses on traditional trades and crafts. There are resident crafts people who currently include a woodcarver, glass designer and felt maker. Temporary exhibitions feature the work of regional artists and crafts people. Please phone for full details.

Birmingham

The Barber Institute of Fine Arts, University of Birmingham, Edgbaston, Birmingham, B15 2TS
tel (0121) 414 7333 *fax* (0121) 414 3370
website www.barber.org.uk *e-mail* info@barber.org.uk

Birmingham (Barber Institute)

Described by the *Observer* as 'one of the finest small galleries in Europe', the Institute's permanent collection comprises Old Master and modern paintings, drawings and sculpture, including major works by Bellini, Rubens, Poussin, Gainsborough, Rossetti, Monet, Renoir and Magritte.

- ■ Braco Dimitrijevic: Triptychos Posthistoricus* To 20 Jan 02
- ■ Puvis de Chavannes 19 Apr – 14 July 02
- ➤ Anthony van Dyck: 'Ecce Homo' and 'The Mocking of Christ'* 25 Oct 02 – 19 Jan 03

    ➤ *Art Museum, Princeton University* ➤ *National Gallery of Ireland, Dublin* ➤ *Courtauld Gallery, London* ➤ *Barber Institute of Fine Arts, Birmingham*

Birmingham Museum & Art Gallery, Chamberlain Square, Birmingham, B3 3DH
tel (0121) 303 2834
website www.birmingham.gov.uk/bmag

The collection includes fine and applied art from the Middle Ages to the present. Among the highlights are 18th- and 19th-century English watercolours, paintings, sculpture, stained glass and drawings by the Pre-Raphaelites, and the Water Hall Gallery of Modern Art, showing 20th- and 21st-century works from Birmingham's collections.

- ■ Living Proof: The Four Galleries Exhibition To Jan 02
- ➤ British Gas Wildlife Photographer of the Year To Jan 02
    Originated by Natural History Museum, London
- ■ Cultural Exchange: Part of the Japan 2001 Festival To 3 Mar 02
- ■ Kunisada and the Japanese Actor Print To 3 Mar 02

Birmingham (Museum)

- Friends of Birmingham Museum & Art Gallery — To Mar 02
- Passion and Perfection – Eric Clements: Silver and Design 1950–1992 — 27 Jan – 14 Apr 02
- Rouault's Miserere — 16 Mar – 13 Aug 02
- Time and Motion — 12 May – 1 Sept 02
- Minoans and Mycenaeans — June – Sept 02

Craftspace Touring, Unit 1/208, Custard Factory, Gibb Street, Birmingham, B9 4AA
tel (0121) 608 6668 *fax* (0121) 608 6669
e-mail info@craftspace-touring.co.uk

➤ A Sense of Occasion: Significant Objects marking Special Occasions in Contemporary Britain* — To 10 Mar 02
  ➤ *The Bowes Museum, Barnard Castle* ➤ *20–20 One, Scunthorpe*
➤ Ikons of Identity: The Contemporary Mask* — To 18 June 02
  ➤ *Durham Light Infantry Museum* ➤ *Scarborough Art Gallery* ➤ *City Museum & Art Gallery, Leicester*
➤ Coming To Our Senses: Multi-Sensory Craft Exhibition* — 28 Jan 02 – 16 Feb 03
  ➤ *The Bracknell Gallery* ➤ *Summerlee Heritage Park, Coatbridge* ➤ *Russell-Cotes Art Gallery & Museum, Bournemouth* ➤ *Newport Museum & Art Gallery*

The Custard Factory, Gibb Street, Digbeth, Birmingham, B9 4AA
tel (0121) 604 7777 *fax* (0121) 604 8888
website www.custardfactory.com *e-mail* post@custardfactory.com
The Custard Factory features a diverse programme of visual and performing arts events and exhibitions. Please phone or consult the website for full details of current exhibitions.

Birmingham

Ikon Gallery, 1 Oozells Square, Brindleyplace,
Birmingham, B1 2HS
tel (0121) 248 0708 *fax* (0121) 248 0709
website www.ikon-gallery.co.uk
e-mail art@ikon-gallery.co.uk
Opening hours are 11:00–6:00 Tuesday–Sunday and Bank Holiday Mondays. Admission is free.

- Braco Dimitrijevic and Richard Hamilton — To 27 Jan 02
- Katharina Grosse and Santiago Sierra — 12 Feb – 7 Apr 02
- Graham Gussin — 16 Apr – 2 June 02
- Jean Frederic Schnyder — 12 June – 21 July 02
- Vladimir Arkhipov and Hayley Newman — 30 July – 8 Sept 02

MAC, Cannon Hill Park, Birmingham, B12 9QH
tel (0121) 440 4221 *fax* (0121) 446 4372
website mac-birmingham.org.uk
e-mail enquiries@mac-birmingham.org.uk
The Midlands Arts Centre hosts over thirty exhibitions each year, and is one of the very few galleries which gives equal space to contemporary fine art, craft and photography, from both established artists and newcomers. Please phone or consult the website for full details.

- ➤ Art Textiles 2 — To 6 Jan 02
  Originated by Bury St Edmunds Art Gallery
- Prints by Mila Judge-Furstova — To 6 Jan 02
- Contemporary Japanese Painting — 12 Jan – 3 Mar 02
- Changing Face: Photographs of the Bullring Project by Luke Unsworth — 12 Jan – 3 Mar 02
- New York Rhythm: Photographs by Silas Wood — 12 Jan – 3 Mar 02
- Mitate: Prints by Nana Shiomi — 19 Jan – 10 Mar 02

➤ Mount Fuji: Photographs by Chris 19 Jan – 10 Mar 02
Steele-Perkins
➤ *MAC, Birmingham* ➤ *Gainsborough's House, Sudbury*

Blackburn
Blackburn Museum & Art Gallery, Museum Street, Blackburn, Lancashire, BB1 7AJ
tel (01254) 667130 *fax* (01254) 695370
website blackburnworld.com
e-mail stephen.whittle@blackburn.gov.uk
The permanent collection includes displays of manuscripts, icons, Japanese prints, artists' books and coins. There are also 19th–20th century paintings and sculpture, ceramics, and an award-winning South Asian gallery. Please phone or consult the website for full details of current exhibitions.

- Layers of Elegance: Kimono through the Ages — To 23 Feb 02
- Peter Cunliffe: Abstract Paintings — 23 Feb – 13 Apr 02
- Paper Planet by Barry Bermange* — 20 Apr – 15 June 02
- John L. Chapman: Watercolours* — 3 Aug – 28 Sept 02
- Durgesh Srivastava: Har Har Ganges* — 21 Sept – 16 Nov 02

Bletchley
Fenny Lodge Gallery, 76 Simpson Road, Fenny Stratford, Bletchley, Milton Keynes, Buckinghamshire, MK1 1BA
tel (01908) 639494 *fax* (01908) 648431
website www.fennylodge.co.uk
e-mail sophie@fennylodge.demon.co.uk
The Gallery offers an extensive collection of contemporary ceramics by leading and lesser known ceramicists, including stoneware, porcelain, terracotta and earthenware. The work of over fifty potters

is on display, and there are two clay exhibitions per year, in April/May and November. Please phone or consult the website for full details.

Bolton

Bolton Museum, Art Gallery & Aquarium, Le Mans Crescent, Bolton, West Yorkshire, BL1 1SE
tel (01204) 332194 *fax* (01204) 332241
website www.boltonmuseums@bolton.gov.uk
e-mail art.gallery@bolton.gov.uk
One of the largest regional art galleries in the North-West, with one of the finest collections of contemporary ceramics in the country. It also houses a large number of watercolours and drawings, and has a significant collection of British-based prints and 20th-century sculpture. Please phone for full details of current exhibitions.

Bournemouth

Russell-Cotes Art Gallery & Museum, East Cliff, Bournemouth, Dorset, BH1 3AA
tel (01202) 451800 *fax* (01202) 451851
website www.russell-cotes.bournemouth.gov.uk
e-mail info@russell-cotes.demon.co.uk
The core of the Russell-Cotes' permanent collection of fine art comprises an important range of Victorian and Edwardian paintings, prints and sculpture, and decorative art from around the world. Please phone or consult website for full details of current exhibitions.

- Floating World, Netsuke* — To 10 Feb 02
- Arts Council Collection* — To Mar 02
  Originated by Oriel Mostyn, Llandudno

Bournemouth (Russell-Cotes) > Bradford

- ■ South London Gallery Collection mid-Apr – July 02
  Exhibition*
- ➤ Coming To Our Senses: Multi-Sensory 12 Aug – 1 Dec 02
  Craft Exhibition*
  ➤ Bracknell Art Gallery ➤ Summerlee Heritage Park, Coatbridge ➤ Russell-Cotes Art Gallery & Museum, Bournemouth ➤ Newport Museum & Art Gallery
  Originated by Craftspace Touring, Birmingham

Bracknell

The Bracknell Gallery, South Hill Park Arts Centre, Ringmead, Bracknell, Berkshire, RG12 7PA
tel (01344) 484858
website www.southhillpark.org.uk
e-mail visualart@southhillpark.org.uk
Please phone or consult the website for full details of current exhibitions.

- ➤ Coming To Our Senses: Multi-Sensory 27 Jan – 29 Apr 02
  Craft Exhibition*
  ➤ The Bracknell Gallery ➤ Summerlee Heritage Park, Coatbridge ➤ Russell-Cotes Art Gallery & Museum, Bournemouth ➤ Newport Museum & Art Gallery
  Originated by Craftspace Touring, Birmingham

Bradford

Cartwright Hall Art Gallery, Lister Park, Bradford, West Yorkshire, BD9 4NS
tel (01274) 751212 *fax* (01274) 481045
website www.bradford.gov.uk
e-mail cartwright.hall@bradford.gov.uk
Cartwright Hall was built in the Baroque style in 1904. Its historic

Bradford (Cartwright Hall)

galleries contain changing displays drawn from its collections of 19th- and 20th-century British art. A new permanent display focuses on the work of artists of south Asian origin or descent. Please phone or consult the website for full details of current exhibitions. Open 10:00–5:00 Tuesday–Saturday, 1:00–5:00 Sunday. Admission free.

- ■ The 20th Century and All That — To Jan 02
- ■ Yorkshire Union of Artists Celebration — To Jan 02
- ■ The Power, the Pride, the Passion: Ian Beesley — To Jan 02
- ➤ Chandrika: Indian Silver Jewellery — 23 Feb – 21 Apr 02
  ➢ *Oldham Gallery* ➢ *Harris Museum, Preston* ➢ *Cartwright Hall*

The Colour Museum, Perkin House, Providence Street, Bradford, West Yorkshire, BD1 2PW
tel (01274) 390955 *fax* (01274) 392888
website www.sdc.org.uk *e-mail* museum@sdc.org.uk
Please phone or consult the website for full details of current exhibitions.

- ■ Feeling Colour: British Polymer Clay Guild Exhibition — Mar – May 02
- ■ Mixed Media by Philip O'Reilly — Sept 02
- ■ A Textile Spectrum: Suzann Thompson — Oct – Dec 02

The National Museum of Photography, Film & Television, Bradford, BD1 1NQ
tel (01274) 202030
website www.nmpft.org.uk *e-mail* talk.nmpft@nmsi.ac.uk
In addition to four special exhibitions per year, the NMPFT houses a unique collection across three media, including images, equipment and ephemera, with a new facility – Insight: The Research Centre – offering access to items not on display in the permanent galleries.

Admission is free, though there may be a charge for special exhibitions. Please phone or consult the website for full details.

Brecon
Brecknock Museum & Art Gallery, Captain's Walk, Brecon, Powys, LD3 7DW
tel (01874) 624121 *fax* (01874) 611281
e-mail brecknock.museum@powys.gov.uk

■ Brecon Theatre: An Historical Celebration	To 26 Jan 02
■ Matthew Richardson: Prints and Works on Paper	To 2 Feb 02
■ Woven Structures by Sue Hiley Harris	To 9 Mar 02
➤ Capel-y-Ffin to Ditchling: Watercolours and Drawings by Edgar Holloway*	9 Feb – 14 Apr 02

  ➣ *Ditchling Museum* ➣ *National Museum of Wales, Aberystwyth*
  ➣ *Brecknock Museum & Art Gallery* ➣ *Tunbridge Wells Museum & Art Gallery* ➣ *Bankside Gallery, London*

■ The Tower on the Hill: Paintings and Drawings by Clive Hicks-Jenkins	16 Mar – 21 Apr 02
■ Recent Art Acquisitions	27 Apr – 7 June 02
■ The Welsh Group	15 June – 27 July 02
■ Brecon Jazz Festival Exhibition: Paintings by Ursula Bayert	3 Aug – 8 Sept 02
■ Welsh Sampler Show	14 Sept – 16 Nov 02
■ Marcelle Davies: Embroideries	Oct 02
■ Kwong Kuen-Shan: Chinese Brush Paintings of Wales	From 23 Nov 02

Brighouse
Smith Art Gallery, Halifax Road, Brighouse, West Yorkshire, HD6 2AF
tel/fax (01484) 719222

Brighouse (Smith Gallery) > Brighton

The gallery's collection comprises 19th-century narrative and landscape paintings, including works by Atkinson Grimshaw, Marcus Stone, J. F. Herring and Philip Hermogenes Calderon. Please phone for full details.

Brighton
Brighton Museum & Art Gallery, Church Road, Brighton, East Sussex, BN1 1UE
tel (01273) 290900 *fax* (01273) 292841

- ■ Kiss and Kill: Film Visions of Brighton* To 7 Apr 02
- ■ Sacred and Profane* 4 May – 30 June 02
- ➤ Nicola Hicks: Sculpture and Drawings 20 July – 15 Sept 02
  ➤ *Brighton Museum & Art Gallery* ➤ *Galway Arts Centre*
- ■ Double Take: Jon Mills Metalwork and Michele Walker Textiles* 28 Sept – 16 Nov 02
- ■ Photograph and Memory: A Seaside Album* 7 Dec 02 – 9 Feb 03

Brighton University Gallery, Grand Parade, Brighton, East Sussex, BN2 2JY
tel (01273) 643010 *fax* (01273) 643038
website www.ac.uk/hubs/news/gallery.html
All exhibitions are free and open to the public 10:00–5:00 Monday to Saturday. (NB times of Annual Show of Graduates' Work vary: Saturday 10:00–6:00, Sunday 12:00–6:00, Monday–Wednesday 10:00–8:00, Thursday 10:00–4:00.)

- ■ Satoru Shoji: Sculptural Installation 14 Jan – 9 Feb 02
- ■ Annual Show of Second Year Work 4 – 27 Mar 02
- ■ Mayo Bucher Apr 02
- ■ Grace Robertson May 02
- ■ Annual Show of Graduates' Work June 02

Brighton (University Gallery) > Bristol

- MA Fine Art Final Year Show — July 02
- Sara Gadd — Aug 02
- MA Sequential Design/Illustration Annual Show — Sept 02
- visions2002: The Festival of International Animated Theatre — Oct 02
- Tony Wilson: Printmaking and Painting — Nov 02
- School of Architecture & Design Annual Show — Dec 02

Gardner Arts Centre Gallery, University of Sussex, Brighton, East Sussex, BN1 9RA
tel (01273) 685861
website www.gardnerarts.co.uk
The Arts Centre Gallery specialises in contemporary art, specifically 3-dimensional exhibitions and installations. Opening hours are 10:00–7:00 Monday–Saturday (except Bank Holidays). Please phone or consult the website for full details of current exhibitions.

Bristol

Arnolfini, 16 Narrow Quay, Bristol, Avon, BS1 4QA
tel (0117) 929 9191 *fax* (0117) 925 3876
website www.arnolfini.demon.co.uk
e-mail arnolfini@arnolfini.demon.co.uk
The Arnolfini presents developments and trends in the visual arts. Its programme of exhibitions draws attention to new British artists as well as celebrating the work of major international artists. Please phone or consult the website for full details of current exhibitions. Open 10:00–7:00 Monday–Wednesday and Friday–Saturday, 10:00–9:00 Thursday, and 12:00–7:00 Sunday and Bank Holiday Mondays.

Bristol > Burnley

Bristol Museum & Art Gallery, Queen's Road, Bristol,
Avon, BS8 1RL
tel (0117) 922 3571 *fax* (0117) 922 2047
website www.bristol-city.gov.uk
e-mail general_museum@bristol-city.gov.uk
The fine art collection comprises paintings, drawings, watercolours, prints and sculptures. Some two hundred oil paintings are usually on display. British artists represented include Reynolds, Gainsborough, Hudson, Rysbrack, Lear, Burne-Jones, Sickert, Frink, Ben Nicholson and Richard Long. Please phone for full details of current exhibitions.

Watershed, 1 Canon's Road, Bristol, Avon, BS1 5TX
tel (0117) 927 6444 *fax* (0117) 921 3958
website www.watershed.co.uk
Please phone or consult the website for full details of current exhibitions.

- Breathe: Hannah Gal — To 20 Jan 02
- Images of Safety: Laura Chessin — 22 Jan – 17 Mar 02
- Animated Encounters — 19 Mar – 28 Apr 02
- Holiday Snaps: Catherine Large & Tom Marshman — 30 Apr – 23 June 02
- ImagineAsian — 20 Aug – 13 Oct 02

Burnley

Towneley Hall Art Gallery & Museums, Burnley,
Lancashire, BB11 3RQ
tel (01282) 424213 *fax* (01282) 436138
website www.burnley.gov.uk/towneley
e-mail towneleyhall@burnley.gov.uk
Collections include furniture, ceramics, glass, sculpture, paintings and watercolours. The fine art collections are particularly strong in

19th-century British works, including paintings by Burne-Jones, John William Waterhouse and Sir Lawrence Alma-Tadema. Please phone or consult the website for full details of current exhibitions. Open 10:00–5:00 Monday–Friday, 12:00–5:00 Sunday. Admission is free.

Bury

Bury Art Gallery & Museum, Moss Street, Bury,
Greater Manchester, BL9 0DR
tel (0161) 253 5878 *fax* (0161) 253 5915
website www.bury.gov.uk/culture.htm *e-mail* artgallery@bury.gov.uk
The permanent collection comprises Victorian paintings and water-colours by such artists as Turner, Constable, Landseer, Cox, Linnell and Stanfield, and 20th-century works by Lowry, Burra, Pasmore and others. Royal Lancastrian pottery and Wedgwood are also well represented. Please phone for full details of current exhibitions.

- ■ 'A Work of Art in Itself': Crafts Exhibition celebrating the Gallery Building — To 19 Jan 02
- ■ Manchester Academy of Fine Arts 143rd Annual Open Exhibition — 23 Mar – 11 May 02
- ■ Schober meets Turner: A Comparison of Light* — 21 Sept – 9 Nov 02

Buxton

Buxton Museum & Art Gallery, Terrace Road, Buxton,
Derbyshire, SK17 6DA
tel (01298) 24658 *fax* (01298) 79394
website www.derbyshire.gov.uk/libraries&heritage
The gallery's permanent collection principally comprises 19th- and early-20th century landscapes and portraits in a variety of media.

- ■ Susan McCall — To 5 Jan 02

Buxton (Museum) > Cambridge

- Charles Monkhouse — To 19 Jan 02
- Kate Bellis: On the Edge — To 23 Feb 02
- Kate Bellis: Idyll – Photographs of Rural Deprivation — 12 Jan – 16 Mar 02
- Permanent Collection — 26 Jan – 9 Mar 02
- R. Procter — 2 Mar – 13 Apr 02
- ➤ Paintings of Derbyshire by Lewis Noble* — 16 Mar – 11 May 02
  - ➤ *Derby Museum & Art Gallery* ➤ *Buxton Museum & Art Gallery*
- Bad Nauheim: Roses — 23 Mar – 27 Apr 02
- Permanent Collection — 20 Apr – 1 June 02
- Landscapes: Jane Fielder — 4 May – 29 June 02
- Derbyshire Open Art Exhibition* — 25 May – 20 July 02
- Buxton & High Peak Art Society — 6 July – 31 Aug 02
- Portraiture: Simon Ashurst — 27 July – 21 Sept 02
- Buxton Community School — 7 Sept – 2 Nov 02
- Su Kyung Yu Friedel — 28 Sept – 23 Nov 02
- Print Works: Natasha Kumar — 9 Nov 02 – 4 Jan 03
- Cheshire Textile Group — 30 Nov 02 – 25 Jan 03

Cambridge

Cambridge Contemporary Art, 6 Trinity Street, Cambridge, CB2 1SU
tel (01223) 324222 *fax* (01223) 315606
website www.artcambridge.co.uk
e-mail cam.cont.art@dial.pipex.com
The permanent collection includes paintings, sculpture, prints and crafts. Artists represented include Craigie Aitchinson, Eoghan Bridge, Chagall, Jonathan Clarke, Charlotte Cornish, Stanley Dove, Elisabeth Frink, Terry Frost, John Hoyland, Albert Irvin, Anita Klein, Karolina Larusdottir, Matisse, Picasso, John Piper, Ray Richardson, Dorothy Stirling, Richard Tuff and Robin Welsh.

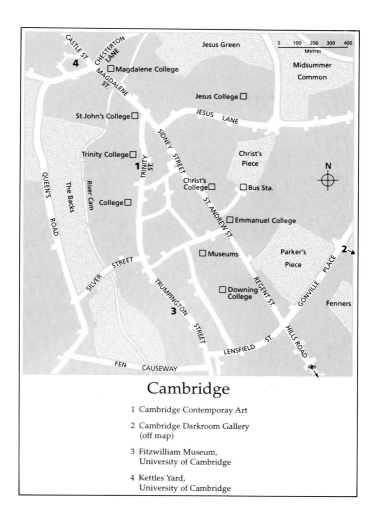

Cambridge

1. Cambridge Contemporay Art
2. Cambridge Darkroom Gallery (off map)
3. Fitzwilliam Museum, University of Cambridge
4. Kettles Yard, University of Cambridge

Cambridge (Contemporary Art)

- Sale: Mixed Exhibition — 2 – 31 Jan 02
- Flair: Mixed Exhibition — 9 – 28 Feb 02
- Ross Loveday Paintings & Blandine Anderson Stoneware — 8 – 30 Mar 02
- Mixed Exhibition: Ellen Bell Mixed Media & Aaronson Noon Glass — 2 – 20 Apr 02
- Pip Carpenter Collagraphs, Susie Perring Etchings and Shakespeare Glass — 26 Apr – 18 May 02
- Mixed Exhibition: Nicola Slattery Prints and Paintings, David Carter Bronzes & Virginia Dowe Ceramics — 21 May – 5 June 02
- Stanley Dove Sculpture & Modern Masters — 7 – 29 June 02
- Mixed Exhibition — 6 – 31 July 02
- Mixed Exhibition: Charlotte Cornish Paintings and Majolica Ceramics — 3 – 31 Aug 02
- Alisia Hyslop Paintings & Eoghan Bridge Sculpture — 6 – 28 Sept 02
- Karolina Larusdottir Watercolours & Trevor Price Handmade Prints — 11 Oct – 2 Nov 02
- Mixed Exhibition — 6 – 30 Nov 02
- Christmas Exhibition — 2 – 24 Dec 02

The Fitzwilliam Museum, Trumpington Street, Cambridge, CB2 1RB
tel (01223) 332900 *fax* (01223) 332923
website www.fitzmuseum.cam.ac.uk
e-mail fitzmuseum-enquiries@lists.cam.ac.uk
The Fitzwilliam's collection includes antiquities, pottery and glass, Oriental art, illuminated manuscripts, drawings, watercolours and prints; and paintings by artists such as Martini, Veneziano, Titian,

Veronese, Rubens, Van Dyck, Hals, Canaletto, Hogarth, Gainsborough, Constable, Monet, Degas, Renoir, Cézanne and Picasso. As a result of development work, from January 2002 until mid–2003 only the Founder's Building will be open. Please consult the website for further information.

Kettle's Yard, Castle Street, Cambridge, CB3 0AQ
tel (01223) 352124 *fax* (01223) 324377
website www.kettlesyard.co.uk *e-mail* mail@kettlesyard.co.uk
Kettle's Yard House includes paintings by Ben and Winifred Nicholson, Christopher Wood and David Jones, and sculpture by Hepworth, Brancusi and Gaudier-Brzeska. The adjacent gallery presents exhibitions of contemporary and modern art. Please phone or consult the website for full details. The Gallery is open 11:30–5:00 all year round, the House 1:30–4:30 30 March–26 August, 2:00–4:00 27 August–29 March. Admission is free.

- Flights of Reality   12 Jan – 3 Mar 02
- Ben Nicholson   27 July – 2 Oct 02

Cannock

Cannock Library, Manor Avenue, Cannock,
Staffordshire, WS11 1AA
tel (01543) 510366 *fax* (01543) 510373
e-mail cannock.library@staffordshire.gov.uk
The gallery is closed January–March for refurbishment.

- Abstract Expressionist Painting: Apr 02
  R. Thursfield
- Mixed Medium Paintings: L. Stanton   May 02
- Cannock Chase Arts Council   June 02
- Figurative Art: S. Buckler   Aug 02
- Watercolours: S. Beardmore   Sept 02

Cannock (Library) > Canterbury

- Paintings: G. Benton — Oct 02
- Cannock Photographic Society — Nov 02

Canterbury

The Herbert Read Gallery, Kent Institute of Art and Design, New Dover Road, Canterbury, Kent, CT1 3AN
tel (01227) 769371 *fax* (01227) 817500 *e-mail* bferrell@kiad.ac.uk
The Herbert Read Gallery hosts a changing programme of contemporary art exhibitions to complement and enhance the courses at each campus, which cover fine art, architecture, modelmaking, fashion, jewellery and time-based media. Please phone for full details of current exhibitions.

The Royal Museum & Art Gallery, High Street, Canterbury, Kent, CT1 2RA
tel (01227) 452747 *fax* (01227) 455047
website www.canterbury-artgallery.co.uk
The permanent collection of fine and decorative art includes work by Gainsborough, Tissot, Epstein, Henry Moore, Laura Knight, Carel Weight and John Ward. Please phone or consult the website for full details of current exhibitions. Admission is free.

- Rollie McKenna: Artists and Writers
  Originated by the National Portrait Gallery, London
- ➤ Edward Ardizzone: Etchings and Lithographs — 23 Mar – 19 May 02
  ➢ *Wakefield Art Gallery* ➢ *Durham Art Gallery* ➢ *Royal Museum & Art Gallery, Canterbury*
  Originated by Wolseley Fine Arts, London
- John Titchell RA: Garden Paintings — 25 May – 13 July 02
- East Kent Art Society — 20 July – 10 Aug 02
- Canterbury Society of Art — 17 Aug – 1 Sept 02

Cardiff

Martin Tinney Gallery, 6 Windsor Place, Cardiff,
South Glamorgan, CF10 3BX
tel (02920) 641411 *fax* (02920) 641422
website www.artwales.com *e-mail* mtg@artwales.com
The Martin Tinney Gallery features a changing programme of exhibitions of work by emerging artists and Wales' leading 20th-century and contemporary artists. Please phone or consult the website for full details of current exhibitions.

National Museum & Gallery, Cathays Park, Cardiff,
South Glamorgan, CF10 3NP
tel (02920) 397951 *fax* (02920) 373219
website www.nmgw.ac.uk *e-mail* post@nmgw.ac.uk
The National Museum's permanent collections include British and European fine art ranging from the 16th to the 19th centuries, including works by Old Masters, Pre-Raphaelites Gwen and Augustus John, and French Impressionists Cézanne, Rodin and Renoir. There is also an impressive collection of sculpture and ceramics.

- ■ Flight* — To 24 Feb 02
- ■ Augustus and Gwen John — To Mar 02
- ■ Richard Wilson at Work — To Apr 02
- ■ Piranesi Prints — Mar – June 02
  Originated by Whitworth Art Gallery, Manchester
- ■ Recreations: Facing the Past — Apr – Sept 02
- ➤ Art in Exile: Flanders, Wales and the First World War — June – Sept 02
  In collaboration with Gent Museum
- ➤ Ceri Richards* — July – Oct 02
  ➤ *National Museum & Gallery, Cardiff* ➤ *Glynn Vivian Art Gallery, Swansea*

Cardiff (National Museum) > Chelmsford

- ■ Spirit   Sept – Nov 02
- ■ Women and Watercolours   Sept – Dec 02
- ■ Star Trek: Federation Science   Nov 02 – Apr 03

Carlisle
Tullie House Museum & Art Gallery, Castle Street, Carlisle, Cumbria, CA3 8TP
tel (01228) 534781 *fax* (01228) 810249
website www.tulliehouse.co.uk

The gallery holds important collections of fine and decorative arts, including paintings and drawings by local and British artists, a substantial body of Pre-Raphaelite work, and porcelain, costume and textiles. Please phone or consult the website for full details of current exhibitions.

- ➤ Winifred Nicholson   To 12 Jan 01
  Originated by Kettle's Yard, Cambridge
- ➤ Antony Gormley's 'Field for the British   18 Jan – 17 Mar 02
  Isles'
  NTE from the Hayward Gallery, London
- ■ Ken Currie   23 Mar – 19 May 02
- ➤ The Snake in the Garden: Contemporary   1 June – 14 July 02
  Approaches to Slipware*
  ➢ *Collins Gallery, Glasgow* ➢ *Victoria Art Gallery, Bath* ➢ *Tullie House Museum & Art Gallery, Carlisle*
  Originated by Aberystwyth Arts Centre

Chelmsford
Chelmsford Central Library, County Hall, Market Road, Chelmsford, Essex, CM1 1LH
tel (01245) 492758 *fax* (01245) 492536
e-mail cfdlib@e1.essexcc.gov.uk

Chelmsford (Central Library)

Please phone for full details of current exhibitions.

- Wil Hilton — To 6 Jan 02
- John Johnston — 2 – 30 Jan 02
- Joyce Gosling — 9 – 30 Jan 02
- Fiona Gates-McQuaid — 2 – 27 Feb 02
- Liz Innocent — 2 – 27 Feb 02
- David Marshall — 2 – 30 Mar 02
- Aytac Uzmen — 2 – 30 Mar 02

Chelmsford & Essex Museum, Oaklands Park, Moulsham Street, Chelmsford, Essex, CM2 9AQ
tel (01245) 615100 *fax* (01245) 611250
website www.chelmsfordbc.gov.uk/museums/index-shtml
e-mail oaklands@chelmsfordbc.gov.uk

The museum's permanent collection includes fine and decorative arts, ceramics, glass, costume and coins, as well as displays of local and social history and natural history. Parking and admission are free. Wheelchair access to ground floor only. Please phone for full details of current exhibitions.

- ➤ British Gas Wildlife Photographer of the Year — To 20 Jan 02
  Originated by the Natural History Museum, London
- Badges and Devices — 26 Jan – 17 Mar 02
- Toybox! — 24 Mar – 9 June 02
- Lynton Lamb, Artist and Illustrator 1907–1977* — 15 June – 1 Sept 02
- The Admiral, the Lion Tamer and the Suffragette: A Scrapbook of Chelmsford People — 14 Sept – 1 Dec 02
- The Guild of Essex Craftsmen — 7 Dec 02 – 26 Jan 03

Cheltenham

Cheltenham Art Gallery & Museum, Clarence Street, Cheltenham, Gloucestershire, GL50 3JT
tel (01242) 237431 *fax* (01242) 262334
website www.cheltenhammuseum.org.uk
e-mail artgallery@cheltenham.gov.uk

A world-famous collection relating to the Arts and Crafts Movement, including furniture, textiles, ceramics, carvings, silver and jewellery. There are also British and Dutch paintings spanning some three hundred years, plus rare Chinese and English ceramics and exhibitions celebrating the social history of Cheltenham.

■ Gloucestershire Guild of Craftsmen	To 13 Jan 02
■ Discovering Nature: The Nature Notebooks of Edward Wilson (1872–1912)	To 3 Mar 02
■ Cheltenham Camera Club	19 Jan – 10 Feb 02
■ Cheltenham Schools Art	16 Feb – 13 Mar 02
➤ Handbags* *Originated by Leicester City Art Gallery*	16 Mar – 28 Apr 02
■ Cheltenham Art Club	4 – 26 May 02
➤ The Man Who Drew Pooh: The Art of E. H. Shepherd* ➢ *Cheltenham Art Gallery & Museum* ➢ Guildford House Gallery, Guildford	9 Mar – 12 May 02
■ The Art of Ladybird Books*	1 June – 25 Aug 02
■ The Arts and Crafts of Chipping Camden	18 May – 14 July 02
■ Play in Cheltenham	22 July – 8 Sept 02
■ Two Drawing Shows	31 Aug – 8 Sept 02
■ African Collections Exhibition	9 Nov 02 – end Jan 03

Chesterfield

Chesterfield Museum & Art Gallery, St Mary's Gate, Chesterfield, Derbyshire, S41 7TD
tel (01246) 345727
e-mail museum@chesterfieldbc.gov.uk
The permanent collection comprises paintings, drawings and sketches spanning the career of locally-born artist Joseph Syddall, who worked mostly in London. Please phone for full details of current exhibitions.

Chichester

Chichester Centre of Arts, St Andrew's Court, East Street, Chichester, West Sussex, PO19 1YH
tel (01243) 779103

■ Invited Members of the Royal Institute of Painters in Watercolours*	7 – 26 Jan 02
■ Winter Open Art Exhibition	10 – 23 Feb 02
■ Annie Thimothy Art Exhibition	2 – 9 Mar 02
■ Photography and Paintings Exhibition on the theme of 'Patterns'	7 – 20 Apr 02
■ Spring Open Art Exhibition	6 – 18 May 02
■ African Rock Art	1 – 8 June 02
■ New Park Artists	4 – 13 July 02
■ City Art Group	15 – 20 July 02
■ Ken Walch Art Exhibition	22 – 27 July 02
■ Chichester Camera Club Photographic Exhibition	29 July – 10 Aug 02
■ Stride & Son Open Art Competition and Exhibition	12 – 24 Aug 02
■ Autumn Open Art Exhibition	7 – 18 Oct 01

Chichester (Centre of Arts) > Christchurch

- City Art Group　　　　　　　　　　　18 – 23 Nov 02
- African Rock Art　　　　　　　　　　26 – 30 Nov 02
- Fourteen Artists Exhibition　　　　　2 – 14 Dec 02

Pallant House Gallery, 9 North Pallant, Chichester,
West Sussex, PO19 1TJ
tel (01243) 774557 *fax* (01243) 536038
website www.pallanthousegallery.com *e-mail* pallant@pallant.co.uk
The Gallery is home to an important collection of modern art, including work by Frank Auerbach, Patrick Caulfield, Barbara Hepworth, Henry Moore, Paul Nash, Ben Nicholson, Pablo Picasso, Ceri Richards, Walter Sickert and Graham Sutherland. Please phone or consult the website for full details of current exhibitions. Open 10:00–5:00 Tuesday–Saturday, 12:30–5:00 Sunday and Bank Holidays.

- Michael Ayrton: Verlaine Suite　　　18 Jan – 17 Mar 02

Christchurch

Red House Museum & Art Gallery, Quay Road, Christchurch, Dorset, BH23 1BU
tel (01202) 482860 *fax* (01202) 481924
website www.hants.gov.uk/museum/redhouse

- The Shoe Show　　　　　　　　　　　12 Jan – 20 Apr 02
  Originated by Hampshire Museums Service
- Discover Gamelan　　　　　　　　　　4 May – 22 June 02
- Christchurch Arts Guild Annual Show　6 – 24 July 02
- Christchurch Scrapbook: Photographic
  Local History Exhibition　　　　　　　3 Aug – 8 Sept 02
- Open Country: Wood Engravings, -　　14 Sept – 6 Oct 02
  Watercolours and Drawings by
  Howard Phipps

Christchurch (Red House) > Cockermouth

- Bournemouth Arts Club   12 Oct – 2 Nov 02
- Verwood Pottery & Heathland Crafts   9 – 22 Dec 02

Cinderford
Dean Heritage Centre, Camphill, Soudley, Forest of Dean, Gloucestershire, GL14 2UB
tel (01594) 822170 *fax* (01594) 823711
e-mail deanmuse@btinternet.com
Please phone for full details of current exhibitions.

Coatbridge
Ironworks Gallery, Summerlee Heritage Park, Heritage Way, Coatbridge, Strathclyde, ML5 1QD
tel (01236) 431261 *fax* (01236) 440429
An extensive collection of documents, photographs and memorabilia pertaining to social and industrial history, plus objects from domestic, commercial and industrial settings, including operational machinery. Please phone for full details of current exhibitions.

Cockermouth
Castlegate House Gallery, Cockermouth, Cumbria, CA13 9HA
tel/fax (01900) 822149
website www.castlegatehouse.co.uk
e-mail gallery@castlegatehouse.co.uk
Established in a Georgian house with Adam ceiling, the gallery specialises in northern and Scottish artists, including Barbara Rae, Percy Kelly, Michael Bennett, Bill Peascod, Sheila Fell, Kurt Jackson, Charles Oakley, Jim Malone and William Plumptre. There are changing exhibitions of stone, ceramic, metal and glass pieces in the walled garden. Please phone for full details of current exhibitions.

Coleraine

Riverside Gallery, Riverside Theatre, University of Ulster, Cromore Road, Coleraine, Northern Ireland, BT52 1SA
tel (02870) 323232 *fax* (02870) 324924
Please phone for full details of current exhibitions.
- Contrasts: John Johnson*   5 – 31 Oct 02

Conwy

Royal Cambrian Academy, Crown Lane, Conwy, LL32 8AN
tel/fax (01492) 593413
website www.rcaconwy.org *e-mail* rca@rcaconwy.org
Opening times are 11:00–5:00 Tuesday–Saturday, 1:00–4:30 Sunday.
- David Loten and David Lloyd-Griffith   12 Jan – 10 Feb 02
- Aneurin Jones and John Meirion Morris   16 Feb – 17 Mar 02
- Jack Shore and Colin See-Paynton   23 Mar – 21 Apr 02
- Will Roberts   27 Apr – 26 May 02
  Originated by the National Library of Wales
- Royal Institute of Painters in Watercolours 1 – 30 June 02
- 120th Annual Summer Exhibition   6 July – 15 Sept 02
- Ken Elias and Isabel McWhirter   21 Sept – 20 Oct 02
- Mike Knowles and Emma Knowles   26 Oct – 24 Nov 02
- Members' Winter Show and Craft   30 Nov – 21 Dec 02

Cookham-on-Thames

Stanley Spencer Gallery, Cookham High Street, Cookham-on-Thames, Berkshire, SL6 9SJ
tel (01628) 471885
website www.stanleyspencer.org *e-mail* diana.benson@ntlworld.com
The gallery presents a permanent collection of Spencer's work together with letters, documents and memorabilia. The gallery also displays important works on long-term loan, and mounts a winter

and summer exhibition each year. Open daily 10:30–5:30 Easter–October, but on weekends and Bank Holidays only, 11:00–5:00, between November and Easter.

Coventry

Herbert Art Gallery & Museum, Jordan Well, Coventry, West Midlands, CV1 5QP
tel (024) 7683 2381 *fax* (024) 7683 2410
website www.coventrymuseum.org.uk
e-mail ann.walker@coventry.gov.uk
The permanent collection includes Graham Sutherland's working drawings for the famous Coventry Cathedral tapestry, portraits of Lady Godiva through the centuries, and 20th-century British art. Please phone or consult the website for full details of current exhibitions.

- Traces: Photographs by Ulli Ull   16 Feb – 12 May 02
- The Homes of Football: Photographs by   8 June – 21 July 02
  Stuart Clarke

Mead Gallery, Warwick Arts Centre, University of Warwick, Coventry, West Midlands, CV4 7AL
tel (02476) 524524 *fax* (02476) 524525
website www.warwickartscentre.co.uk
e-mail box.office@warwick.ac.uk
Please phone or consult the website for full details of current exhibitions.

Croydon

Croydon Clocktower, Museum & Cultural Services Heritage Service, Croydon Clocktower, Katharine Street, Croydon, Greater London, CR9 1ET

Croydon (Clocktower) > Darlington

tel (020) 8253 1022 *fax* (020) 8253 1003
website www.croydon.gov.uk/clocktower
e-mail exhibitions@croydon.gov.uk
The gallery houses an extensive collection of Chinese pottery and ceramics. Please phone or consult the website for full details of current exhibitions.

- ■ 'Wonderful World of Bollywood': The To Jan 02
  Music, Fashion and Film of India*

Darlington
Darlington Art Gallery, Crown Street, Darlington,
County Durham, DL1 1NB
tel (01325) 462034

- ■ J. Paterson: Exhibition of Oils Jan 02
- ■ Camera Club Exhibition of Photographs Feb 02
- ■ Tricia McLaughlin Mar 02
- ■ Rita Smith Apr 02
- ■ Exhibition of Work by A-Level Students at May 02
  Darlington Sixth Form College
- ■ Exhibition of Work by Art Foundation June 02
  Course Students at Darlington Sixth
  Form College
- ■ Lisa House: Abstract and Colour July 02
  Experimentation
- ■ G. Beveridge Aug 02
- ■ Joint Exhibition of Work by Four Local Sept 02
  Artists: B. Watson, M. Shotton, W. Lancaster
  and T. Furness
- ■ Darlington Society of Arts Annual Exhibition 5 – 26 Oct 02
- ■ Dover Prize Annual Art Competition Dec 02

Denbigh > Derby

Denbigh

Denbigh Library, Museum & Art Gallery, Church Street, Rhyl, LL18 3AA
tel (01745) 353814 *fax* (01745) 331438
e-mail manan.edwards@denbighshire.gov.uk
Please phone for full details of current exhibitions.

Derby

Derby Museum & Art Gallery, The Strand, Derby, DE1 1BS
tel (01332) 716659 *fax* (01332) 716670
website www.derby.gov.uk/museums
e-mail jderbyshire@derbymuseum.freeserve.co.uk
The permanent collection includes fine and decorative arts, Derby porcelain and 18th-century paintings by Joseph Wright of Derby.

- ■ Sustainable Design and Practice* 12 Jan – 24 Feb 02
- ➤ Paintings of Derbyshire by Lewis Noble* 19 Jan – 10 Mar 02
    - ➤ *Derby Museum & Art Gallery* ➤ *Buxton Museum & Art Gallery*
- ■ Paintings by David Manley* 23 Mar – 5 May 02
- ■ Local Arts Festival 9 Mar – 21 Apr 02
- ■ Collections Exhibition 9 Mar – 21 Apr 02
- ■ Paintings by Anthony Currell* 4 May – 16 June 02
- ■ Jubilation Exhibition: Celebrations in Derby 29 June – 18 Aug 02
- ➤ The Mare's Tale: Nursery Rhymes Explored through Various Media* 13 July – 1 Sept 02
    - ➤ *Drumcroon Art & Education Centre, Wigan* ➤ *Hereford Museum & Art Gallery* ➤ *Derby Museum & Art Gallery* ➤ *Bristol Museum & Art Gallery*
    - *Originated by Bury Art Gallery & Museum*
- ■ Evelyn Williams Fellowship Retrospective* 31 Aug – 20 Oct 02
- ■ Derby City Open Art Exhibition 16 Nov 02 – 5 Jan 03

Derby > Donaghadee

Q Gallery, 35/36 Queen Street, Derby, DE1 3DS
tel (01332) 295858
website www.q-arts.co.uk *e-mail* create@q-arts.co.uk
Q Gallery displays a range of contemporary art by local, regional and national artists, many of whom use photography and new media in their work.

- Pets Don't Buy Things: Photographs by Paul Hill* 23 Jan – 23 Feb 02
- Listening to Young People 2: by Young People from Derby 6 Mar – 6 Apr 02
  In collaboration with National Children's Bureau
- Best in Show: Best Work by Graduates from the East Midlands Region 17 Apr – 18 May 02
  In collaboration with the East Midlands Arts Board

Derry

Context Gallery, The Playhouse, 5–7 Artillery Street, Derry, Northern Ireland, BT48 6RG
tel (02871) 373538 *fax* (02871) 261884
website www.contextgallery.com *e-mail* info@contextgallery.com
The gallery organises twelve exhibitions each year. Its aims are to encourage and promote emerging Irish artists, and to develop links with artists in other countries. Shows in 2002 include Irish architecture awards, public art by Ruth Jones, Emma Donaldson, and themed shows on Joyce's *Ulysses* and the trope of the Palindrome. Please phone or consult the website for full details of current exhibitions.

Donaghadee

Cleft Art Gallery, 3 Markethouse, New Street, Donaghadee, Co. Down, Northern Ireland, BT21 0AG *tel* (02891) 888502

Original oil paintings, watercolours, mixed media, charcoal and pencil drawings by leading Irish artists, including Tom Kerr, Ian Darragh, Hamilton Sloan, Darren Paul, Glynnis Burns, Iuan Frew, Paul Cunningham, Ken Hamilton, Paul Watson, Esther Brimage and Conor Fleck.

Doncaster

Doncaster Museum & Art Gallery, Cheque Road, Doncaster, South Yorkshire, DN1 2AE
tel (01302) 734293 *fax* (01302) 735409
website www.doncaster.gov.uk *e-mail* museum@doncaster.gov.uk

- ■ The Doncaster Dome: Janet Samson — To 17 Feb 02
- ■ Sea Coalers: Photographic Exhibition — 16 Feb – 14 Apr 02
  Originated by the National Coalmining Museum, Wakefield
- ■ David Venables — 23 Feb – 21 Apr 02
- ■ Doncaster Art Club — 4 May – 30 June 02
- ■ Doncaster Camera Club — 11 May – 7 July 02
- ■ Made in China* — 15 June – 11 Aug 02
- ■ The Dockin Hill Years: Doncaster School of Arts and Crafts — 6 July – 1 Sept 02
- ■ Janet Buckle — 7 Sept – 3 Nov 02
- ■ Don Jacklin — 14 Sept – 10 Nov 02

Dublin

City Arts Centre Gallery, 23/25 Moss Street, Dublin 2, Ireland
tel (00 353 1) 677 0643 *fax* (00 353 1) 677 0131
website homepage.eircom.net/~cityarts
e-mail cityartscentre@eircom.net

The gallery provides an opportunity to view a large cross-section of work, ranging from education or community–based projects to established artists, issue-based work, and young artists exhibiting for the first time. Please phone or consult the website for full details of current exhibitions.

Douglas Hyde Gallery, Trinity College, Nassau Street, Dublin 2, Ireland
tel (00 353 1) 608 1116 *fax* (00 353 1) 670 8330
website www.douglashydegallery.com
e-mail dhgallery@tcd.ie
Please phone or consult the website for full details of current exhibitions.

Irish Museum of Modern Art, Royal Hospital, Military Road, Kilmainham, Dublin 8, Ireland
tel (00 353 1) 612 9900 *fax* (00 353 1) 612 9999
website www.modernart.ie *e-mail* info@modernart.ie
Ireland's leading national institution devoted to modern and contemporary art, with a dynamic programme of exhibitions which regularly include bodies of work from its own permanent collection. Please phone or consult the website for full details. Open 10:00–5:30 Tuesday–Saturday, 12:00–5:30 Sunday and Bank Holidays. Admission is free.

■ Sol LeWitt: New Wall Drawings	To 27 Jan 02
■ Irish Art Now: From the Poetic to the Political	To Mar 02
■ A Collection Show	To Apr 02
■ Gordon Lambert Collection	22 Jan – June 02
■ Rowan Collection	6 Feb – June 02
■ Irish Projects Exhibition	27 Feb – 26 May 02
■ Ann Hamilton	28 Mar – 30 June 02
■ Thomas Ruff	19 July – 28 Oct 02

Dublin (Irish Museum)

- ➤ Imaging Ulysses: Richard Hamilton's 7 June – 15 Sept 02
  Illustrations to James Joyce
  - ➤ *British Museum, London* ➤ *Irish Museum of Modern Art, Dublin*
- ■ Willie Doherty 20 Nov 02 – Feb 03

Kerlin Gallery, Anne's Lane, South Anne Street, Dublin 2, Ireland
tel (00 353 1) 670 9093 *fax* (00 353 1) 670 9096
website www.kerlin.ie *e-mail* gallery@kerlin.ie
Artists represented include Chung Eun-Mo, Barrie Cooke, Dorothy Cross, Willie Doherty, Felim Egan, Mark Francis, David Godbold, Elizabeth Magill, Brian Maguire, Stephen McKenna, Fionnuala Ni Chiosáin, Kathy Prendergast, Sean Scully and Séan Shanahan. Open 10:00–5:45 Monday–Friday, 11:00–4:30 Saturday. Please phone or consult the website for full details of current exhibitions.

National Gallery of Ireland, Merrion Square (West), Dublin 2, Ireland
tel (00 353 1) 661 5133 *fax* (00 353 1) 676 6488
website www.nationalgallery.ie *e-mail* artgall@eircom.net
The National Gallery of Ireland's permanent collection includes oil paintings, drawings, watercolours, prints, sculptures and *objets d'art*. As well as Irish historic paintings and European Old Masters, it houses a fine collection of British paintings, and is the home of the Irish national portrait collection and the Yeats Museum. Please phone or consult the website for full details of current exhibitions.

- ■ Monet, Renoir and the Impressionist mid Jan – Apr 02
  Landscape*
  Originated by the Museum of Fine Arts, Boston
- ■ Terbrugghen's 'Crucifixion'* Feb – May 02
  Originated by the Metropolitan Museum of Modern Art, New York

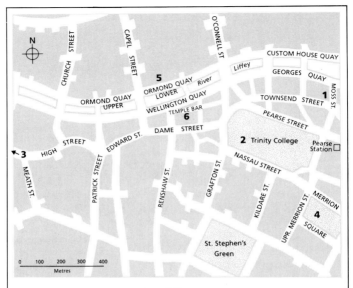

Dublin

1 City Arts Centre Gallery

2 The Douglas Hyde Gallery

3 The Irish Museum of Modern Art (off map)

4 The National Gallery of Ireland

5 Ormond Multimedia Gallery

6 Temple Bar Gallery and Studios

Dublin (National Gallery)

- American Beauty: Painting and Sculpture　　June – Aug 02
  from the Detroit Museum of Arts
  1770–1920*
  National Gallery of Ireland, Dublin ➤ Van Gogh Museum, Amsterdam
  Originated by the Detroit Museum of Arts
- Anthony van Dyck: 'Ecce Homo' and　　　19 June – 11 Aug 02
  'The Mocking of Christ'*
  Art Museum, Princeton University ➤ National Gallery of Ireland, Dublin ➤ Courtauld Gallery, London ➤ Barber Institute of Fine Arts, Birmingham
- Jules Breton*　　　　　　　　　　　　　15 Sept – end Nov 02
  Musée de Beaux-Arts, Arras ➤ Musée des Beaux-Arts, Quimper ➤ National Gallery of Ireland, Dublin

Royal Hibernian Academy, Gallagher Gallery, 15 Ely Place, Dublin 2, Ireland
tel (00 353 1) 661 2558 *fax* (00 353 1) 661 0762
website www.royalhibernianacademy.com
e-mail rhagallery@eircom.net
An artist-based and artist-orientated institution that has promoted the fine arts in Ireland since 1823. Please phone or consult the website for full details of current exhibitions.

Rubicon Gallery, 1st Floor, 10 St Stephen's Green, Dublin 2, Ireland
tel (00 353 1) 670 8055 *fax* (00 353 1) 670 8057
e-mail rubicongallery@iol.ie
The Rubicon Gallery shows contemporary paintings, drawings and sculpture by Irish and international artists, with some twelve to fourteen solo exhibitions and two to three themed group shows every year. Please phone for full details of current exhibitions.

Dublin (Rubicon) > Dumfries

- Samuel Walsh — 8 Jan – 3 Feb 02
- Michael Kane — 5 Feb – 3 Mar 02
- Patrick M. Fitzgerald — 5 – 31 Mar 02
- Maud Cotter — 9 Apr – 5 May 02
- Chen Zhongsen — 7 May – 2 June 02
- Maire Hanlon — 3 – 29 Sept 02
- Anita Groener — 1 – 27 Oct 02
- Alexis Harding — 29 Oct – 24 Nov 02
- Eithne Jordan — 26 Nov – 22 Dec 02

Solomon Gallery, Powerscourt Townhouse Centre, South William Street, Dublin 2, Ireland
tel (00 353 1) 679 4237 *fax* (00 353 1) 671 5262
website www.solomongallery.com *e-mail* solomon.gallery@indigo.ie
Gallery artists and sculptors include Brian Ballard, John Bellany, Colin Davidson, Ana Duncan, Rowan Gillespie, Leo Higgins, Desmond Kinney, Therese McAllister, Hector McDonnell, Victor Richardson, Sarah Spackman and Imogen Stuart. Please phone or consult the website for full details of current exhibitions.

Dudley

Dudley Museum & Art Gallery, St James's Road, Dudley, West Midlands, DY1 1HU
tel (01384) 815571 *fax* (01384) 815576
Open 10:00–4:00 Monday–Saturday. The gallery shows a variety of exhibitions specialising in local history. Please phone for full details.

Dumfries

Gracefield Arts Centre, 28 Edinburgh Road, Dumfries, DG1 1NW
tel (01387) 262084 *fax* (01387) 255173
website www.dgc.gov.uk

Dumfries (Gracefield) > Dundee

The Arts Centre is home to five hundred works of art by Scottish artists with connections to Dumfries and Galloway from the 1840s to the present day, including E. A. Taylor, John Maxwell McTaggart, Joan Eardley, Alan Davie, Barbara Rae and Elizabeth Blackadder. Please phone or consult the website for full details of current exhibitions.

- Jilly Edwards Tapestries — 5 Jan – 2 Feb 02
  Originated by Brewery Arts Centre, Kendal
- Young Blood 2002: Art Graduates from D&G* — 9 Feb – 16 Mar 02
- Gracefield Permanent Collection — 23 Mar – 17 Apr 02
- Dumfries Camera Club Annual Exhibition — 23 Mar – 18 May 02
- Inuit Art — 20 Apr – 18 May 02
  Originated by Narwhal Arts
- Chris J. Ferguson Retrospective* — 25 May – 29 June 02
- No Small Feat* — 25 May – 29 June 02
  Originated by Street Level Gallery, Glasgow
- Dumfries and Galloway Fine Art Society* — 6 July – 3 Aug 02
- International Printmaking Exhibitions and Summer School* — 10 Aug – 14 Sept 02

Dundee

Duncan of Jordanstone College of Art & Design, 13 Perth Road, Dundee, Tayside, DD1 4HT
tel (01382) 345330 *fax* (01382) 345192
website www.exhibitions.dundee.ac.uk
e-mail exhibitions@dundee.ac.uk
Five galleries showing works in fine art, new media, design and architecture. Please phone or consult the website for full details of current exhibitions.

Dundee > Durham

McManus Galleries, Albert Square, Dundee, Tayside, DD1 1DA
tel (01382) 432084 *fax* (01382) 432052
website www.dundeecity.gov.uk
e-mail arts.heritage@dundeecity.gov.uk
One of Scotland's most impressive collections of fine and decorative art, including Victorian and 20th-century Scottish painting and work by Pre-Raphaelite artists such as Millais and Rossetti. Open 10:30–5:00 Monday–Saturday, 10:30–7:00 Thursday, 12:30–4:00 Sunday. Closed 25/26 December and 1/2 January. Full disabled access.

- Celebration of Colour — To 13 Jan 02
- Prohibition — To 20 Jan 02
- Royal Scottish Watercolour Society — 2 Feb – 16 Mar 02
- Life at Liff — Apr – June 02
- ➤ British Gas Wildlife Photographer of the Year — 29 June – 21 Sept 02
  Originated by Natural History Museum, London
- Cinderella's Slipper — 5 Oct 02 – 5 Jan 03

Durham

DLI Museum & Durham Art Gallery, Aykley Heads, Durham DH1 5TU
tel (0191) 384 2214 *fax* (0191) 386 1770
website www.durham.gov.uk/dli
e-mail durham.gallery@durham.gov.uk
Open daily, 10:00–4:00 November–March, 10:00–5:00 April–October.

- ➤ Cartoons from the Permanent Collection
  travelling from Victoria Art Gallery, Bath
- ➤ Ikons of Identity: The Contemporary Mask — To 20 Jan 02
  - ➤ *DLI Museum & Durham Art Gallery* ➤ *Scarborough Art Gallery*
  - ➤ *City Museum & Art Gallery, Leicester*
  Originated by Craftspace Touring, Birmingham

Durham (DLI)

- ➤ Magic of Masks and Puppets — To 20 Jan 02
  - ➢ *DLI Museum & Durham Art Gallery* ➢ *Mansfield Museum & Art Gallery* ➢ *Rhyl Library, Museum & Art Gallery*
  - *Originated by the Scottish Masks & Puppet Centre*
- ➤ Edward Ardizzone: Etchings and Lithographs — 2 Feb – 10 Mar 02
  - ➢ *Wakefield Art Gallery* ➢ *Durham Art Gallery* ➢ *Royal Museum & Art Gallery, Canterbury*
  - *Originated by Wolseley Fine Arts, London*
- ■ Norman Ackroyd: Travels with Copper and Zinc — 16 Mar – 21 Apr 02
- ■ Looking in Wonderland: Drawings by John Tenniel — 16 Mar – 21 Apr 02
- ■ Strangely Familiar: Philip Cox Sculptures — 27 Apr – 2 June 02
- ■ Rich Man, Poor Man, Beggar Man, Thief: Cartoons from the last 100 Years — 27 Apr – 2 June 02
- ■ Coalfield: Contemporary Photographs of Northern Landscapes — 8 June – 21 July 02
- ■ Art for All — 27 July – 8 Sept 02
- ■ Cathedral Artist in Residence — 14 Sept – 27 Oct 02
- ■ Anecdotal Eye: Wood Engravings by Thomas Bewick — 14 Sept – 27 Oct 02
- ■ Eurocrafts — 2 – 10 Nov 02
- ■ Durham Open — 16 Nov – 8 Dec 02

Durham University Oriental Museum, Elvet Hill, Durham, DH1 3TH
tel/fax (0191) 374 7911
website www.dur.ac.uk *e-mail* orientalmuseum@durham.ac.uk
The museum displays collections from ancient Egypt to Japan, South-East Asia and the Islamic world, including a gallery dedicated entirely to China. There is also a lively schedule of temporary

exhibitions displaying contemporary arts and crafts. Full disabled access. Please phone or consult the website for full details.

- Tibet in Photographs by Mike Trickett   Jan 02
- Contemporary Thangkas by Rakhee Sharma   Jan 02

Eastbourne

Towner Art Gallery & Local Museum, High Street, Old Town, Eastbourne, East Sussex, BN20 8BB
tel (01323) 411688 *fax* (01323) 648182
website www.eastbourne.org
e-mail townergallery@eastbourne.gov.uk
The permanent collection consists mainly of 19th–20th-century British art, including work by Lawrence Alma Tadema, Frances Hodgkins, Henry Moore and William Nicholson, with a gallery devoted to Eric Ravilious. Please phone or consult the website for full details of current exhibitions. Open 12:00–5:00 Tuesday–Saturday April–October, 12:00–4:00 November–March, and 2:00–5:00 Sundays and Bank Holiday Mondays. Closed Good Friday, 24–27 December and 1 January.

- Towner Collection Show   To Apr 02

Edinburgh

Art Edinburgh, 20a Dundas Street, Edinburgh, EH3 6HZ
tel/fax (0131) 557 5002
website www.art-scotland.com/www.art-edinburgh.com
e-mail theedinburghgallery@btinternet
This new gallery, which opened in June 2000, houses contemporary Scottish art. There is no wheelchair access.

- Howard Coles   9 Mar – 2 Apr 02
- Jacqueline Marr   1 – 25 June 02

Edinburgh (Art Edinburgh)

- Geoff Uglow   3 – 17 Aug 02
- New Graduates   7 – 24 Sept 02
- Geoff Roper   26 Oct – 19 Nov 02
- Christmas Exhibition   30 Nov – 31 Dec 02

Calton Gallery, 10 Royal Terrace, Edinburgh, EH7 5AB
tel (0131) 556 1010 *fax* (0131) 558 1150
website www.caltongallery.co.uk *e-mail* mail@caltongallery.co.uk
The permanent collection includes paintings, watercolours and sculpture by British and European artists from 1750–1940, specialising in Scottish and marine pictures. Please phone for full details of current exhibitions.

City Art Centre, 2 Market Street, Edinburgh, EH1 1DE
tel (0131) 529 3993 *fax* (0131) 529 3977
website www.cac.org.uk
Please phone or consult the website for full details of current exhibitions.

- Quest for Camelot: The Arthurian Legend in Art   To 26 Jan 02
- ➤ The Art of *Star Wars*   23 Mar – 6 Sept 02
    ➤ *Helsinki City Art Museum* ➤ *City Art Centre, Edinburgh*
    Originated by the Barbican Art Gallery, London

Collective Gallery, 22–28 Cockburn Street, Edinburgh, EH1 1NY
tel (0131) 220 1260 *fax* (0131) 220 5585
website www.collectivegallery.co.uk
e-mail collgall@aol.com
Please phone or consult the website for full details of current exhibitions.

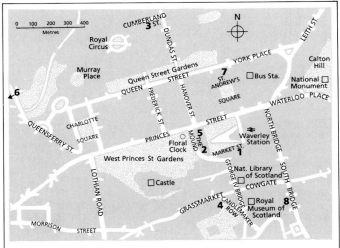

Edinburgh

1. City Art Centre
2. National Gallery of Scotland
3. The Open Eye Gallery
4. Portfolio Gallery
5. Royal Scottish Academy
6. Scottish National Gallery of Modern Art (off map)
7. Scottish National Portrait Gallery
8. Talbot Rice Gallery

Edinburgh

Dean Gallery, Belford Road, Edinburgh, EH4 3DS
tel (0131) 624 6200 *fax* (0131) 343 3250
website www.natgalscot.ac.uk
e-mail enquiries@natgalscot.ac.uk
The Dean Gallery provides a home for the Eduardo Paolozzi gift of sculpture and graphic art, the Gallery of Modern Art's renowned Dada and Surrealist collections, and a major library and archive centre.

- ■ Beuys to Hirst: Art Works at Deutsche Bank — To 13 Jan 02
- ➤ Nigel Henderson: Parallel of Life and Art — 16 Feb – 7 Apr 02
  - ➤ *Graves Art Gallery, Sheffield* ➤ *Dean Gallery, Edinburgh*
- ■ Howard Hodgkin Aug – Oct 02

The Edinburgh Gallery, 18a Dundas Street, Edinburgh, EH3 6HZ
tel/fax (0131) 557 5227
website www.art-scotland.com/www.art-edinburgh.com
e-mail theedinburghgallery@btinternet
A small, independent gallery which specialises in contemporary Scottish art. There is no wheelchair access.

- ■ Ian Cook and Angela Reilly — 16 Mar – 9 Apr 02
- ■ Gallery Stock — July 02
- ■ Geoff Uglow — 3 – 17 Aug 02
- ■ Selection of Scottish Paintings — 19 Aug – 3 Sept 02
- ■ Mixed continued — 7 – 24 Sept 02
- ■ Christmas Exhibition — 30 Nov – 31 Dec 02

The Fruitmarket Gallery, 45 Market Street, Edinburgh, EH1 1DF
tel (0131) 225 2383 *fax* (0131) 220 3130
website www.fruitmarket.co.uk *e-mail* info@fruitmarket.co.uk
One of Scotland's foremost venues for national and international contemporary art, with a wide-ranging exhibition programme of

Edinburgh (Fruitmarket)

national and international art which highlights, in particular, the work of young Scottish artists. Please phone for full details of current exhibitions.

Ingleby Gallery, 6 Carlton Terrace, Edinburgh, EH7 5DD
tel (0131) 556 4441 *fax* (0131) 556 4454
website www.inglebygallery.com *e-mail* mail@inglebygallery.com
Gallery artists include David Austen, Jeffrey Blondes, Felim Egan, Ian Hamilton Finlay, Andy Goldsworthy, Howard Hodgkin, Callum Innes, Patricia MacDonald, John McLean, Craig Murray-Orr, Sean Scully, Alison Watt and Emily Young. Open 10:00–5:00 Tuesday–Saturday. Please phone or consult the website for full details of current exhibitions.

- Four Photographers — 6 Feb – 9 Mar 02
- Ian Hamilton Finlay — 20 Mar – 27 Apr 02
- Felim Egan — 8 May – 8 June 02

National Gallery of Scotland, The Mound, Edinburgh, EH2 2EL
tel (0131) 624 6200 *fax* (0131) 343 3250
website www.natgalscot.ac.uk
e-mail enquiries@natgalscot.ac.uk
As well as the national collection of Scottish art, the gallery contains an outstanding collection of paintings, sculpture, drawings, watercolours and prints ranging from the Renaissance to Post-Impressionism, including works by Velazquez, El Greco, Rembrandt, Vermeer, Turner, Constable, Monet and Van Gogh.

- Newly Acquired Drawings in the National Gallery — To 31 Jan 02
- The Vaughan Bequest of Turner Watercolours — 1 – 31 Jan 02
- Rosslyn: Country of Painter and Poet — 19 Apr – 7 July 02

Edinburgh (National Gallery)

- Rubens and Italian Art 14 June – 1 Sept 02
  - *National Gallery of Scotland, Edinburgh* *Djanogly Art Gallery, Nottingham*

National Library of Scotland, George IV Bridge,
Edinburgh, EH1 1EW
tel (0131) 226 4531 *fax* (0131) 622 4803
website www.nls.uk *e-mail* enquiries@nls.uk
A small display of new acquisitions and selected items from the Special and General Collections can be viewed in the Barrel Vaults in the entrance hall. The Library's summer exhibition, listed below, is open 10:00–5:00 Monday–Friday (10:00–8:00 during the Edinburgh Festival in August), 2:00–5:00 Sunday. Admission free.

- From Tom Thumb to J. K. Rowling: 31 May – 31 Oct 02
  A History of Children's Books

The Open Eye Gallery, 75–79 Cumberland Street,
Edinburgh, EH3 6RD
tel/fax (0131) 557 1020
website www.openeyegallery.co.uk
e-mail open.eye@virgin.net
Artists represented by the Open Eye include Leon Morocco, John Bellany, John Brown, Simon Laurie, Archie McIntosh, Gordon Wyllie, Sandy Murphy, Glen Scouller, Chris Bushe and Jock McInnes.

- Thematic Exhibition 5 – 24 Jan 02
- Angus McEwan & Robert Austin 26 Jan – 14 Feb 02
- Kirsty Wither & George Donald 16 Feb – 7 Mar 02
- Mixed Glass Exhibition 16 Feb – 7 Mar 02
- David Martin, Donald Provan & Alison Weightman 9 – 28 Mar 02
- Helen Smythe 9 Mar – 18 Apr 02

Edinburgh (Open Eye)

- Claire Harrigan, Clare Banks & David White — 30 Mar – 18 Apr 02
- Archie Dunbar McIntosh, David Schofield & Mary Brown — 20 Apr – 9 May 02
- John Brown, Colin Black & Liam Flynn — 11 – 30 May 02
- Glen Scouller & Jackie Watt — 1 – 20 June 02
- Alberto Morrocco — 22 June – 11 July 02
- Summer Show — 13 July – 7 Aug 02
- Jeremy James — 13 July – 7 Aug 02
- Chris Bushe & Malcolm Martin — 9 Aug – 5 Sept 02
- Contemporary Scottish Painting — 9 Aug – 5 Sept 02
- Sarah Carrington & Jennifer Pettigrew — 7 – 26 Sept 02
- Jock MacInnes, Paul Barnes & Claire Kalvis — 28 Sept – 17 Oct 02
- Matthew Draper & Jennie Hale — 19 Oct – 7 Nov 02
- Claire Hillerby — 19 Oct – 28 Nov 02
- John Bellany — 9 – 28 Nov 02
- Sculpture — 9 – 28 Nov 02
- On a Small Scale: Mixed Exhibition — 30 Nov – 24 Dec 02
- Deborah Edwards — 30 Nov – 31 Dec 02

Royal Scottish Academy, The Mound, Edinburgh, EH2 2EL
tel (0131) 558 7097 *fax* (0131) 557 6417
website www.royalscottishacademy.org
The Royal Scottish Academy is Scotland's foremost promoter of contemporary art in the fields of painting, sculpture, printmaking and architecture. Its galleries at The Mound will be closed until mid-2003 for major development work. Please phone or consult the website for details of 2002 and 2003 programme of exhibitions, being held at alternative venues.

Edinburgh

Scottish National Gallery of Modern Art, Belford Road,
Edinburgh, EH4 3DR
tel (0131) 624 6200 *fax* (0131) 343 3250
website www.natgalscot.ac.uk *e-mail* enquiries@natgalscot.ac.uk
The gallery's collection of 20th-century painting, sculpture and graphic art includes major works by Caro, Dali, Ernst, Hepworth, Kirchner, Magritte, Matisse, Moore, Picasso and Vuillard among others, plus many Scottish painters and colourists, including Gillies, Mackintosh, Redpath, MacTaggart and Philipson. Please phone or consult the website for full details of current exhibitions.

Scottish National Portrait Gallery, 1 Queen Street,
Edinburgh, EH2 1JD
tel (0131) 624 6200 *fax* (0131) 343 3250
website www.natgalscot.ac.uk *e-mail* enquiries@natgalscot.ac.uk
A visual history of Scotland since the 16th century, told through the portraits of those who shaped it – royals and rebels, poets and philosophers, heroes and villains. The gallery also displays sculptures, coins, medallions, drawings and watercolours, and houses the National Photography Collection.

■ The Fine Art of Photography	To 13 Jan 02
■ A Tribute to Edwin Morgan	To 3 Feb 02
■ Great Houses of Scotland	25 Jan – 21 Apr 02
■ Wolfgang Suschitzky	21 Feb – Apr 02
■ Dumas Egerton Miniatures	22 Mar – 16 June 02
■ Scots in Film: Portraits by Donald Maclellan	May – Sept 02
■ Drummond of Hawthornden	May – Sept 02
■ David Octavius Hill and Robert Adamson	May – Sept 02
■ Ossian: New Work by Calum Colvin	Oct 02 – Jan 03
■ On Top of the World: Scottish Mountaineers at Home and Abroad	25 Oct 02 – 19 Jan 03

Exeter

Exeter Phoenix, Bradninch Place, Gandy Street, Exeter,
Devon, EX4 3LS
tel (01392) 219741 *fax* (01392) 667080
website www.exeterphoenix.org.uk
e-mail admin@exeterphoenix.org.uk
Exhibitions each have an associated workshop. The gallery is open 10:00–5:00 Monday–Saturday, and has full disabled access. Please phone for full details of current exhibitions.

■ Magic Carpet: Twenty-One Years and More	12 Jan – 2 Feb 02
■ Animation Festival	11 – 23 Feb 02
■ Chinks Grills Glass Installation	28 Feb – 22 Mar 02
■ Deborah Law Printmaking	28 Feb – 22 Mar 02
■ South-West Academy of Fine & Applied Arts Children's Exhibition*	26 Mar – 27 Apr 02
■ Landscapes of the Mind	2 – 22 May 02
➤ Society of Wood Engravers 64th Annual Exhibition*	25 May – 18 June 02
■ Mythologies*	22 Aug – 14 Sept 02
■ South-West Academy of Fine & Applied Arts Open Exhibition*	21 Sept – 9 Nov 02
■ Phoenix Christmas Exhibition featuring Laurel Keeley Ceramics*	14 Nov – 14 Dec 02

Royal Albert Memorial Museum, Queen Street, Exeter.
Devon, EX4 3RX
tel (01392) 665858 *fax* (01392) 421252

■ Burmese Lacquer	To 2 Feb 02
■ Exeter Engraved	To 23 Feb 02
■ The Eye That Never Sleeps: Terence Donovan Photographs*	16 Feb – 13 Apr 02

Exeter (Royal Albert) > Falmouth

- St Ives Group   20 Apr – 8 June 02
- ➤ Saving Faces: Portraits by Mark Gilbert   14 Sept – 16 Nov 02
  ➤ *National Portrait Gallery, London* ➤ *City Art Gallery, Leeds* ➤ *Royal Albert Memorial Museum, Exeter*
- Cold Heaven: Don McCullin on Aids in Africa   30 Sept – 1 Dec 02

Falmouth

Falmouth Art Gallery, Municipal Buildings, The Moor, Falmouth, Cornwall, TR11 2RT
tel (01326) 313863 *fax* (01326) 318608
Open 10:00–5:00 Monday–Saturday. Wheelchair access.

- Richard Long and Kurt Jackson: Delabole – The Slate Quarry Show   5 Jan – 2 Feb 02
- John Ward CBE   9 Feb – 16 Mar 02
- Dan Dare & The *Eagle*: The Art of Frank Hampson   23 Mar – 27 Apr 02
- Animal Matters: Ceramics, an International Festival of Clay   4 May – 15 June 02
- Seasides   22 June – 31 Aug 02
- Great Impressions: Contemporary and Modern Master Prints   7 Sept – 12 Oct 02
- ➤ Picasso: Histoire Naturelle   19 Oct 02 – 5 Jan 03
  NTE from Hayward Gallery, London

Falmouth Arts Centre, 24 Church Street, Falmouth, Cornwall, TR11 3EG
tel (01326) 314566 *fax* (01326) 319461
website www.falmoutharts.org *e-mail* poly@falmoutharts.org
The Centre is owned by the Royal Cornwall Polytechnic Society. It has four galleries, which are available for hire whenever the society

Falmouth (Arts Centre) > Farnham

is not mounting one of its own exhibitions. Please phone or consult the website for full details of current exhibitions.

Farnham

CCA Galleries (Farnham), 13 Lion and Lamb Yard, West Street, Farnham, Surrey, GU9 7LL
tel (01252) 722231 *fax* (01252) 733336
website www.ccagalleries.com *e-mail* farnham@ccagalleries.com
Contemporary prints, paintings, ceramics, glass, sculpture and jewellery. Please phone or consult the website for full details of current exhibitions.

New Ashgate Gallery, Wagon Yard, Farnham, Surrey, GU9 7PS
tel (01252) 713208 *fax* (01252) 737398
website www.newashgategallery.com
e-mail gallery@newashgate.co.uk

- ■ 'One Hundred': Paintings and Prints priced at £100 — 5 Jan – 2 Feb 02
- ■ New Work by Sandra Blow — 9 Feb – 9 Mar 02
- ➤ Recent Graduates — 16 Mar – 13 Apr 02
    - ➤ *New Ashgate Gallery, Farnham* ➤ *Cranleigh Arts Centre*
- ■ Sculpture Show — 20 Apr – 18 May 02
- ■ Outside Sculpture Show at Millais Nurseries — 20 Apr – 22 June 02
- ■ Sonia Lawson — 25 May – 22 June 02
- ■ Summer Show — 29 June – 31 Aug 02
- ■ John Maltby Ceramics and Marj Bond Paintings — 7 Sept – 5 Oct 02
- ■ Jenny Grevatte Paintings — 12 Oct – 9 Nov 02
- ■ Christmas Exhibition — 16 Nov – 31 Dec 02

Fishguard

West Wales Arts Centre, Castle Hill, 16 West Street, Fishguard, Pembrokeshire, SA65 9AE
tel/fax (01348) 873867
website home.btconnect.com/west-wales-arts/
e-mail westwalesarts@bt.connect.com
An extensive collection of contemporary fine art including paintings, drawings, sculpture and crafts. Exhibitions include emerging and established artists from Wales and beyond, often inspired by the Pembrokeshire landscape. Please phone or consult the website for full details.

■ David Tress* Summer 02

Forfar

Forfar Museum & Art Gallery, Meffan Institute, 20 West High Street, Forfar, Tayside, DD8 1BB
tel (01307) 464123 *fax* (01307) 468451
e-mail the.meffan@angus.gov.uk
The gallery houses a growing collection of contemporary work by Scottish artists, a sizeable collection of watercolours, pastels and drawings by James Waterson Herald, and several oils by George Paul Chalmers.

Glasgow

Art Gallery and Museum, Kelvingrove, Glasgow, Strathclyde, G3 8AG
tel (0141) 287 2699 *fax* (0141) 287 2690
Upstairs galleries house an extensive art collection including pieces by Botticelli, Rembrandt, Whistler and 'Glasgow Boys and Girls' such as Melville and Margaret MacDonald. Downstairs are displays

Glasgow (Art Gallery)

of natural history and European arms and armour. Please phone for full details of current exhibitions.
- ■ Adapt Now: Contemporary Group Show   15 Feb – 10 Mar 02

Burrell Collection, Pollok Country Park, Glasgow, Strathclyde, G43 1AT
tel (0141) 287 2550 *fax* (0141) 287 2597
The Burrell Collection, one of the finest in the country, was gifted to the city by shipowner Sir William Burrell in 1944. It excels in Ancient, Oriental and Medieval European art. Please phone for full details of current exhibitions.

Collins Gallery, University of Strathclyde, 22 Richmond Street, Glasgow, Strathclyde, G1 1XQ
tel (0141) 548 2558 *fax* (0141) 552 4053
e-mail collinsgallery@strath.ac.uk
The permanent collection includes over seven hundred paintings and drawings by British artists from 1750 to the present, and over six hundred historic scientific instruments ranging from 1730 to 1950. A catalogue will be available on the web from January 2002.
- ► Art Textiles 2: New Developments in Contemporary Textile Art*   20 Jan – 2 Mar 02
  Originated by Bury St Edmunds Art Gallery
- ■ Terry Setch Retrospective*   9 Mar – 13 Apr 02
  Originated by Howard Gardens Gallery
- ■ Hai Huang: Tale of Two Cities – Contemporary Chinese Watercolours from Glasgow and Suzhou*   20 Apr – 18 May 02
- ■ Ten Thousand Li: Work by British Chinese Lens-based Artists*   20 Apr – 18 May 02
  Originated by the Open Eye Gallery, Liverpool

Glasgow (Collins)

- Boxes: Contemporary Boxes by Master Craftspeople* 1 – 29 June 02
  Originated by Tullie House Museum & Art Gallery, Carlisle
- Mary Maclean: Foiled – Photographs on Aluminium* 6 July – 10 Aug 02
- Making Journeys: Textiles by Inge Hueber, Anne Keith and Veronica Togneri* 17 Aug – 21 Sept 02
- Tom McKendrick: Heavier Than Air – Multi-Media Installation* 5 Oct – 23 Nov 02
- The Collins Christmas Show: Contemporary Applied Art 30 Nov – 21 Dec 02

Gallery of Modern Art, Queen Street, Glasgow, Strathclyde, G1 3AZ
tel (0141) 229 1996 *fax* (0141) 204 5316
GoMA has four main galleries themed on the elements of Air, Earth, Fire and Water, featuring the work of Scottish artists such as Alan Davie, John Byrne and Alison Watt alongside that of international artists such as Eduard Bersudsky.

Hunterian Art Gallery, University of Glasgow, 22 Hillhead Street, Glasgow, G12 8QQ
tel (0141) 330 5431 *fax* (0141) 330 3618
website www.hunterian.gla.ac.uk
e-mail syoung@museum.gla.ac.uk
The gallery's important collection of European paintings includes works by Rembrandt, Koninck, Stubbs and Chardin, portraits by Ramsay and Reynolds, and paintings by 19th–20th-century Scottish artists. The University also owns the world's largest collection of work by Charles Rennie Mackintosh, and the estate of American painter James McNeill Whistler.

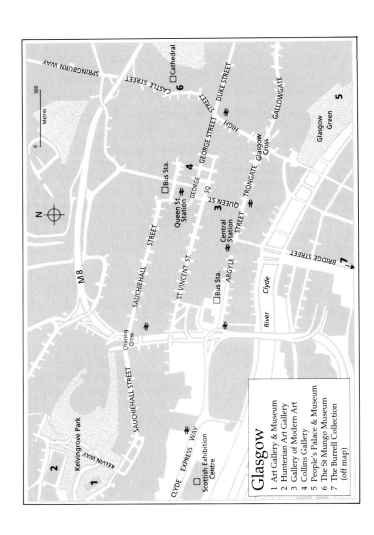

Glasgow (Hunterian)

- ➤ Bridget Riley: Silkscreen Prints and 11 Feb – 15 Apr 02
  Gouaches 1963–2001
  NTE from the Hayward Gallery, London
- ■ The Caracci and Printmaking in Bologna Jan – June 02
  1550–1650
- ■ The Scottish Colourists June 02 – May 03

McLellan Galleries, 270 Sauchiehall Street, Glasgow,
Strathclyde, G2 3EH
tel (0141) 287 2609
Please phone for full details of current exhibitions.

People's Palace, Glasgow Green, Glasgow, Strathclyde, G40 1AT
tel (0141) 554 0223 *fax* (0141) 554 0892
Please phone for full details of current exhibitions.

Royal Glasgow Institute of the Fine Arts, 5 Oswald Street,
Glasgow, Strathclyde, G1 4QR
tel (0141) 248 7411 *fax* (0141) 221 0417
e-mail enquiries@robbferguson.co.uk
Please phone for full details of current exhibitions.
- ■ 141st Annual Exhibition of the Royal 27 Oct – 17 Nov 02
  Glasgow Institute of the Fine Arts*

Royal Scottish Society of Painters in Watercolour,
5 Oswald Street, Glasgow, Strathclyde, G1 4QR
tel (0141) 248 7411 *fax* (0141) 221 0417
website www.rsw-exhibition.com
e-mail enquiries@robbferguson.co.uk
- ■ The Royal Scottish Society of Painters in 3 Feb – 17 Mar 02
  Watercolour 122nd Annual Exhibition*

Glasgow > Greenock

St Mungo's Museum of Religious Life & Art, 2 Castle Street,
Glasgow, Strathclyde, G4 0RH
tel (0141) 553 2557 *fax* (0141) 552 4744
Please phone for full details of current exhibitions.

Gloucester
Gloucester City Museum & Art Gallery, Brunswick Road,
Gloucester, GL1 1HP
tel (01452) 524131 *fax* (01452) 410898
website www.mylife.gloucester.gov.uk
e-mail lindac.@glos-city.gov.uk
Collections include special displays of Queen Anne furniture, ceramics, and paintings by such artists as Turner and Gainsborough. Open all year 10:00–5:00 Monday–Saturday (Sundays 10:00–4:00 July–September only). Please phone or consult the website for full details of current exhibitions.

- ➤ Quilt Art: Moving On*   16 Mar – 13 Apr 02
  Originated by the Royal Cornwall Museum, Truro
- ■ Exhibition of Work by P. J. Crook   20 Apr – 1 June 02
- ■ Cheltenham Group of Artists   24 Sept – 2 Nov 02
- ■ Gloucester Society of Artists   9 Nov – 7 Dec 02

Greenock
McLean Museum & Art Gallery, 15 Kelly Street, Greenock,
Strathclyde, PA16 8JX
tel (01475) 715624 *fax* (01475) 715626
website www.inverclyde.gov.uk
e-mail val.boa@inverclyde.gov.uk
Many of the McLean's wide range of displays are linked by a maritime theme. There are also Clyde Pottery ceramics, Greenock provincial silver, and items from China, Oceania and Japan. The art

gallery regularly features the McLean's own fine arts collection. Please phone or consult the website for full details of current exhibitions.

- ➤ Picasso: Histoire Naturelle　　　　　　　12 Jan – 9 Feb 02
  NTE from the Hayward Gallery, London

Guernsey

Guernsey Museum & Art Gallery, Candie Gardens, St Peter Port, Guernsey, Channel Islands, GY1 1UG
tel (01481) 726518 *fax* (01481) 715177
e-mail admin@museum.guernsey.net
Please phone for full details of current exhibitions.

- ■ Charles Coker: Paintings　　　　　　　17 Jan – 1 Apr 02
- ■ Normandy Paintings　　　　　　　　　10 Apr – 26 May 02
  Originated by Conseil Regionale de Basse-Normandie
- ■ Gosselin & Lukis: Watercolours　　　　20 June – Oct 02
- ■ Art from the Gallery Collection　　　　Oct – Dec 02
- ➤ British Gas Wildlife Photographer of the　Dec 02 – Jan 03
  Year
  Originated by the Natural History Museum, London

Guildford

Guildford House Gallery, Guildford House, 155 High Street, Guildford, Surrey, GU1 3AJ
tel (01483) 444740 *fax* (01483) 444742
website www.guildfordhouse.co.uk
e-mail guildfordhouse@remote.guildford.gov.uk
Pastel portraits by John Russell (painter to George III), plus paintings, drawings and prints of Guildford and the surrounding area, 19th–20th-century works by Henry Pether, Henry Prosser, Henry Sage, Edward Wesson and Ronald Smoothey, and a craft

Guildford (Guildford House) > Halifax

collection including ceramics, textiles, embroidery and glass.
Open 10:00–4:45 Tuesday–Saturday. Admission is free.

- ■ With this Ring … Marriage and Weddings 2 Feb – 30 Mar 02
- ■ Taste of Art: Sugarcraft 2 – 30 Mar 02
- ■ Surrey Photographic Association 6 Apr – 11 May 02
- ➤ The Man Who Drew Pooh: The Art of 18 May – 31 Aug 02
  E. H. Shepherd
  ➤ *Cheltenham Art Gallery & Museum* ➤ *Guildford House Gallery, Guildford*
- ■ Access through Art 7 – 28 Sept 02
- ■ Faith Winter: Figurative Sculptures 5 – 26 Oct 02
- ■ Guildford Art Society Annual Exhibition 2 – 23 Nov 02
- ■ Christmas Craftshop by Surrey Guild of 27 Nov – 21 Dec 02
  Craftsmen

Halifax

Bankfield Museum, Boothtown Road, Halifax,
West Yorkshire, HX3 6HG
tel (01422) 352334 *fax* (01422) 349020
website www.calderdale.gov.uk
e-mail bankfieldmuseum@calderdale.gov.uk

An internationally important collection of textiles, costume and crafts from around the world, including contemporary work and site-specific commissions by leading artists and makers such as Sally Greaves Lord, Michael Brennand Wood, Lon Walpole and Heather Belcher.

- ■ 'Collective Response': Work by the To 13 Jan 02
  62 Group*
- ➤ Peugot/Oxo Design Awards* 19 Jan – 17 Mar 02
  Originated by Peugot Design
- ■ Michelle House: Textiles 23 Mar – 19 May 02

- Loop: Textiles and Sculptures by Six Artists* 28 Sept 02 – 14 Jan 03

Piece Hall Art Gallery, Piece Hall, Halifax, West Yorkshire, HX1 1RE
tel (01422) 358087 *fax* (01422) 349310
website www.calderdale.gov.uk *e-mail* the.mill@calderdale.gov.uk
The Gallery's permanent collection includes costume, textiles and decorative arts. Please phone or consult the website for full details of current exhibitions.

- Helen Muspratt: Photographs 26 Jan – 24 Mar 02
- From Source to Sea: Photographs by Ian Beesley 15 Apr – 9 June 02
- Peter Brook: Paintings 15 June – 18 Aug 01
- Illustrators: Images 26 – The Art of the Illustrator 24 Aug – 10 Nov 02
- Christmas Crafts 2002 16 Nov 02 – 14 Jan 03

Harrogate

Chantry House Gallery, Ripley, Harrogate, North Yorkshire, HG3 3AY
tel (01423) 771011
The gallery exhibits a changing array of paintings, prints and limited editions ranging from the traditional to the contemporary, with an emphasis on original work by popular northern artists such as James Naughton, Emerson Mayes and Nel Whatmore. Please phone for full details of current exhibitions.

Hartlepool

Hartlepool Art Gallery, Church Square, Hartlepool, Cleveland, TS24 7EQ
tel (01429) 869706 *fax* (01429) 523477

The gallery's collection includes 19th-century British oil paintings and watercolours, 20th-century paintings, applied art and work by local artists. Its Oriental collections include Chinese *Famille Rose* porcelain and Japanese artwork and armour. Please phone for full details of current exhibitions.

Havant
The Gallery at Havant Arts Centre, East Street, Havant, Hampshire, PO9 1BS
tel (02392) 472700 *fax* (02392) 498577
website www.havarts@dircon.co.uk *e-mail* havarts@dircon.co.uk
The gallery shows various exhibitions of work by local, national and international artists. Please phone or consult the website for full details of current exhibitions.

Hereford
Hereford Museum & Art Gallery, Broad Street, Hereford, HR4 9AU
tel (01432) 260692 *fax* (01432) 342492
website www.herefordshire.gov.uk
e-mail plyoung@herefordshire.gov.uk
Please phone or consult the website for full details of current exhibitions.

- John Everett Drawings, Video and Sculptural Work — To 19 Jan 02
- ➤ The Mare's Tale: Nursery Rhymes Explored through Various Mediums* — 20 Apr – 23 June 02
    ➤ Drumcroon Art & Education Centre, Wigan ➤ Hereford Museum & Art Gallery ➤ Derby Museum & Art Gallery ➤ Bristol Museum & Art Gallery
    Originated by Bury Art Gallery & Museum
- Herefordshire Photography Festival — 14 Sept – 2 Oct 02

Hitchin

Hitchin Museum & Art Gallery, Paynes Park, Hitchin, Hertfordshire, SG5 1EQ
tel (01462) 434476 *fax* (01462) 431316
The Museum and Art Gallery hosts an active programme of temporary exhibitions. Please phone for full details. Open 10:00–5:00 Monday–Tuesday and Thursday–Saturday. There is wheelchair access to the exhibition galleries.

■ Hitchin Art Club*	To 5 Jan 02
■ Janet Thackeray: Watercolour Exhibition	12 Jan – 23 Feb 02
■ Shades: Group Exhibition	12 Jan – 23 Feb 02
■ Hertfordshire Embroiderers' Guild Silver Jubilee Exhibition*	20 Apr – 18 May 02
■ Colour Scape: Group Exhibition*	25 May – 22 June 02
■ Hitchin Sixth Form Art*	29 June – 20 July 02
■ Take Ten Families: Community Exhibition	27 July – 7 Sept 02
■ Hitchin to Howeswater: Investigating the Relationship between Jacob Thompson and Samuel Lucas*	14 Sept – 26 Oct 02
■ Hitchin Art Club*	2 Nov – 7 Dec 02

Holywood

Charles Gilmore Fine Art Dealers, 31 Church Road, Holywood, Co. Down, Northern Ireland, BT18 9BU
tel (02890) 428555 *fax* (02890) 424440
website www.charlesgilmore.com
e-mail charles@charlesgilmore.co.uk
Charles Gilmore Fine Art Dealers specialise in young contemporary artists, including Terry Bradley, Trevor Brown, Justin Vaughan, Joanna Tinsley, Derek Melville, William Cunningham, Lesley Rainey, Pamela Hamilton and Jenny Davidson.

Hove

Hove Museum & Art Gallery, 19 New Church Road, Hove,
East Sussex, BN3 4AB
tel (01273) 290200 *fax* (01273) 292827
website www.brighton-hove.gov.uk
Hove Museum & Art Gallery is closed from July 2001 till Autumn 2002 for redevelopment work. Please phone or consult the website from August 2002 onwards for details of forthcoming exhibitions.

Huddersfield

Huddersfield Art Gallery, Princess Alexandra Walk, Huddersfield,
West Yorkshire, HD1 2SU
tel (01484) 221962 *fax* (01484) 221952
e-mail hudlib.artgal@kirkleesme.gov.uk
Huddersfield Art Gallery hosts chiefly 20th-century British paintings, drawings, prints and sculpture, but with some 19th-century and earlier, plus European works, Japanese prints, contemporary ceramics, and the work of regional landscape painters.

- ➤ Arturo di Stefano: Recent Paintings, Drawings & Prints* 17 Jan – 9 Mar 02
  - ➤ *Huddersfield Art Gallery* ➤ *Worcester City Art Gallery*
- ■ Obsessions: Exhibition by Women Photographers 18 Apr – 15 June 02
- ➤ Spotlight on Kenneth Martin* 8 June – 20 July 02
  NTE from the Hayward Gallery, London
- ■ Staff from Huddersfield University Fine Art Department 19 Sept – 16 Nov 02

Hull

University of Hull Art Collection, University of Hull,
Cottingham Road, Hull, East Riding of Yorkshire, HU6 7RX

tel (01482) 346311 *fax* (01482) 465192
website www.hull.ac.uk/arts/facultyfiles/artcoll.htm
e-mail o.l.macfarlane@hull.ac.uk
This is a small but important collection specialising in British paintings, sculpture, drawings and prints of the period 1890–1940, including work by Beardsley, Epstein, Gaudier-Brzeska, Gill, Augustus John, Henry Moore, Ben Nicholson, Pissarro, Sickert, Spencer and Steer. Also on display are two collections of Chinese ceramics. Please phone or consult the website for full details of current exhibitions.

Inverness
Inverness Museum & Art Gallery, Castle Wynd, Inverness, IV2 3EB
tel (01463) 237114 *fax* (01463) 225293
The permanent collection includes Inverness silver, weapons and bagpipes from the Highlands, and contemporary Scottish art. There is an ever-changing programme of temporary exhibitions. Please phone for details. Open 9:00–5:00 Monday–Saturday. Admission is free.

Ipswich
Wolsey Art Gallery, Christchurch Mansion, Christchurch Park, Soane Street, Ipswich, Suffolk, IP4 2BE
tel (01473) 433554 *fax* (01473) 433564
Christchurch Mansion houses a collection of work by Suffolk artists, including the best collection of Constables and Gainsboroughs outside London, plus a fine collection of British pottery, porcelain and glassware, and 16th–19th-century English furniture in period room settings. Please phone for full details of current exhibitions.

Kelso > Kilkenny

Kelso

Floors Castle, Roxburghe Estates Office, Kelso, Borders, TD5 7SF
tel (01573) 223333 *fax* (01573) 226058
website www.floorscastle.com *e-mail* marketing@floorscastle.com
Floors Castle displays an outstanding collection of French 17th–18th-century furniture, tapestries, Chinese and European porcelain, and many other works of art, much of it collected by the eighth Duke's American wife, Duchess May.

Kendal

Abbot Hall Art Gallery, Kendal, Cumbria, LA9 5AL
tel (01539) 722464 *fax* (01539) 722494
website www.abbothall.org.uk *e-mail* info@abbothall.org.uk
The permanent collection includes watercolours of the Lake District by Turner, Ruskin, Lear, Cotman and others, and modern works by Lucian Freud, Bridget Riley, Ben Nicholson, Frank Auerbach, Stanley Spencer and Kurt Schwitters. Eighteenth-century paintings, miniatures and society portraits, displayed in their period setting alongside furniture and *objets d'art*, include key works by George Romney.

Kilkenny

Butler Gallery, Kilkenny Castle, Kilkenny, Ireland
tel (056) 61106 *fax* (056) 70031
website www.butlergallery.com *e-mail* butlrgal@indigo.ie
The gallery's collection, begun in 1943, provides a creditable account of the evolution of 20th-century art in Ireland, and includes works by such artists as Sir John Lavery, Yeats, Patrick Scott, Tony O'Malley and Dorothy Cross. Please phone or consult the website for full details of current exhibitions.

King's Lynn > Kingston upon Hull

King's Lynn

King's Lynn Arts Centre, 29 King Street, King's Lynn,
Norfolk, PE30 1HA
tel (01553) 779095 *fax* (01553) 766834

The Arts Centre presents at least twelve exhibitions of contemporary art each year, covering all media, plus lectures, workshops, and artists' talks and residencies. Regular events include an annual competition, the Eastern in March–May, the Festival in July–August, and the Christmas Crafts Shop. Free admission. Please phone for full details.

Kingston upon Hull

Ferens Art Gallery, Monument Buildings, Queen Victoria Square, Kingston upon Hull, Humberside, HU1 3RA
tel (01482) 613902 *fax* (01482) 613710
website www.hullcc.gov.uk/museums
e-mail museums@hullcc.gov.uk

The gallery houses a permanent collection of paintings from the 17th century onwards, with an emphasis on Dutch and Flemish artists, portraits, marine painters, 19th- and 20th-century watercolours, and contemporary art. There is also a broad programme of temporary exhibitions. Please phone or consult the website for full details.

➤ Bridget Riley: Silkscreen Prints and Gouaches 1963–2001 *NTE from the Hayward Gallery, London*	To 27 Jan 02
■ Ferens Winter Exhibition*	16 Feb – 21 Apr 02
■ Chris Dobrowolski	May – June 02
■ From Medieval to Regency: Old Masters in the Collection*	22 June – 6 Oct 02

Kirkaldy

Kirkaldy Museum & Art Gallery, War Memorial Gardens, Kirkaldy, Fife, KY1 1YG
tel (01592) 412860 *fax* (01592) 412870
e-mail dallas.tlechan@fife.gov.uk
A collection of fine and decorative arts, including 18th–20th-century Scottish paintings and a large collection of works by William McTaggart and Scottish colourist S. J. Peploe, as well as paintings by Lowry, Sickert, Redpath, Bellany and the 'Glasgow Boys'. Please phone for full details of current exhibitions.
- Flora Celtica   To 6 Jan 02
- Making a Mark: Works on Paper   To 27 Jan 02

Lancaster

City Museum, Market Square, Lancaster, LA1 1HT
tel (01524) 64637 *fax* (01524) 841692
website www.lancaster.gov.uk/museums
e-mail pthompson@lancaster.gov.uk
- Lancaster and District Art Society Show   2 Mar – 13 Apr 02
- Lancaster's Markets: Paintings by Ian Gardner   20 Apr – 25 May 02

Leeds

Bruton Gallery, Trafalgar House, 29 Park Place, Leeds, West Yorkshire, LS1 2SP
tel (0113) 242 2323 *fax* (0113) 242 1447
website www.brutongallery.co.uk *e-mail* art@brutongallery.co.uk
Bruton Gallery specialises in the work of European Master Sculptors, including Auguste Rodin, Aristide Maillol, Emile Antoine Bourdelle, Joseph Bernard, Jules-Aimé Dalou, Robert Wlérick, Michael Ayrton and Henry Moore. It also promotes the paintings and sculpture of

Leeds (Bruton)

many living artists. Please phone or consult the website for full details of current exhibitions.

City Art Gallery, The Headrow, Leeds, West Yorkshire, LS1 3AA
tel (0113) 247 8248 *fax* (0113) 244 9689
website www.leeds.gov.uk

The gallery's nationally designated fine art collections range from the early 19th century to the late 20th, including English watercolours, fine Victorian academic and Pre-Raphaelite painting and late 19th-century French pictures, plus an extensive display of modern sculpture. Please phone or consult the website for full details of current exhibitions.

- ■ Maquettes for Monuments by Jean Dubuffet* — To 6 Jan 02
- ■ Raymond Booth — 7 Feb – 7 Apr 02
- ■ Shine: Sculptures drawn from the Henry Moore Institute Collection — 16 Feb – 12 May 02
- ■ New Collection Displays from the Henry Moore Institute — Mar – Dec 02
- ➤ Mirror Mirror: Self-Portraits by Women Artists — 17 Apr – 9 June 02
  - ➤ *National Portrait Gallery, London* ➤ *City Art Gallery, Leeds* ➤ *Victoria Art Gallery, Bath*
- ■ Drawings by Liesbeth Bik and Jos van der Pol — 8 June – 1 Sept 02
- ➤ Saving Faces: Portraits by Mark Gilbert — 20 June – Aug 02
  - ➤ *National Portrait Gallery, London* ➤ *City Art Gallery, Leeds* ➤ *Royal Albert Memorial Museum, Exeter*
- ■ Leeds Photographic Society: Anniversary Exhibition — Sept 02
- ■ Sculpture/Architecture in Post-War Britain — 3 Oct 02 – 5 Jan 03

Leeds (City Art Gallery)

- 'I don't want to look any more. I just want to see': Photographic Portraiture — mid Oct – Dec 02

Henry Moore Institute, 74 The Headrow, Leeds,
West Yorkshire, LS1 3AH
tel (0113) 246 7267 *fax* (0113) 246 1481
website www.henry-moore.ac.uk *e-mail* liz@henry-moore.ac.uk
The Institute is responsible for the sculpture collections of Leeds Museums & Galleries. These are displayed in the Institute's own galleries, Leeds' City Art Gallery, Temple Newsam and Lotherton Hall. An archive and library are also housed in the Institute.

- Close Encounters: The Sculptor's Studio in the Age of the Camera* — To 6 Jan 02
- Unidentified Museum Objects — To 28 Feb 02
- Second Skin: 19th-Century and Contemporary Life Casting* — 16 Feb – 12 May 02
- Christina Mackie — Mar – May 02
- Sculpture Now — 8 June – 1 Sept 02
- About Face: Masks from the British Museum — June – Sept 02
- Polychromy in English Medieval Sculpture — 3 Oct 02 – 5 Jan 03

The University Gallery Leeds, Parkinson Building,
Woodhouse Lane, Leeds, West Yorkshire, LS2 9JT
tel (0113) 233 2777 *fax* (0113) 233 5561
website www.leeds.ac.uk/library/gall/exhibs.html
e-mail libhmd@library.novell.leeds.ac.uk
The permanent collection comprises 19th- and 20th-century British and European paintings, drawings and prints, including works by the Camden Town and Bloomsbury groups, with small collections

of sculpture and ceramics. Please phone or consult the website for full details of current exhibitions.

Leicester

Belgrave Hall, c/o New Walk Museum, New Walk,
Leicester, LE1 7EA
tel (0116) 247 3042 *fax* (0116) 247 3057
website www.leicestermuseums.ac.uk
e-mail knapsool@leicester.gov.uk
A free exhibition, *The Shape of Things to Come*, is open all year.

The City Gallery, 90 Granby Street, Leicester, LE1 1DJ
tel (0116) 254 0595 *fax* (0116) 254 0593
Concentrating on contemporary art and crafts, the gallery offers a dynamic and accessible programme of exhibitions and events, and runs an active and popular education programme. Please phone for full details of current exhibitions.

Guildhall, Leicester, c/o New Walk Museum, New Walk,
Leicester, LE1 7EA
tel (0116) 247 3042 *fax* (0116) 247 3057
website www.leicestermuseums.ac.uk
e-mail knapsool@leicester.gov.uk
Please phone or consult the website for full details of current exhibitions.

Jewry Wall Museum, c/o New Walk Museum, New Walk,
Leicester, LE1 7EA
tel (0116) 247 3042 *fax* (0116) 247 3057
website www.leicestermuseums.ac.uk
e-mail knapsool@leicester.gov.uk

Leicester (Jewry Wall) > Letchworth

Please phone or consult website for full details of current exhibitions.

Leicester City Museum & Art Gallery, 53 New Walk, Leicester, LE1 7EA
tel (0116) 255 4100 *fax* (0116) 247 3011
website www.leicestermuseums.ac.uk
e-mail knapsool@leicester.gov.uk
The gallery has permanent displays of Victorian and German Expressionist work and decorative art from around the world. The collection includes works by Francis Bacon, Spencer, Hogarth, Lowry, Dicksee, William Dyce, Frith, Franz Marc, William Powell and Kandinsky. Please phone or consult the website for full details of current exhibitions.

New Walk Museum, New Walk, Leicester, LE1 7EA
tel (0116) 247 3042 *fax* (0116) 247 3057
website www.leicestermuseums.ac.uk
e-mail knapsool@leicester.gov.uk
Please phone or consult website for full details of current exhibitions.

Letchworth
Letchworth Museum & Art Gallery, Broadway, Letchworth, Hertfordshire, SG6 3PF
tel (01462) 685647 *fax* (01462) 481879
website www.nhdc.gov.uk
e-mail letchworth.museum@nhdc.gov.uk
Open 10:00–5:00 Monday–Saturday (closed on Wednesdays, Sundays and bank holidays). Please phone or consult the website for full details of current exhibitions.

Lincoln > Liverpool

Lincoln
Usher Gallery, Lindum Road, Lincoln, LN2 1NN
tel (01522) 527980 *fax* (01522) 560165
e-mail usher.gallery@lincolnshire.gov.uk
A major Lincolnshire venue for fine and decorative arts, including watches, clocks, paintings, miniatures, enamels, glass, silver, porcelain, topographical paintings and drawings, and the nationally important Peter de Wint collection. There is also a varied programme of temporary exhibitions. Please phone for details.

- Artist in Residence — 9 Feb – 24 Mar 02
- Brave New World: 1920s Exhibition — 16 Feb – 12 May 02
- Crossover — 6 Apr – 25 May 02
- Portrait of Emotion — 23 May – 30 June 02
- Lincolnshire Artists — 14 Sept – 17 Nov 02
- Travelling Companions — 1 Dec 02 – 2 Feb 03

Liverpool
The Conservation Centre, Whitechapel, Liverpool, L1 6HZ
tel (0151) 478 4999
website www.nmgm.org.uk *e-mail* claire.rider@nmgm.org
The Conservation Centre provides an insight into the world of museum and gallery conservation and shows how conservators preserve and restore everything from fine art and sculpture to spacesuits and archaeological treasures. Open 10:00–5:00 Monday–Saturday, 12:00–5:00 Sunday. Please phone or consult the website for full details of current exhibitions.

Lady Lever Art Gallery, Port Sunlight, Lower Road, Wirral, Merseyside, CH62 4EQ
tel (0151) 478 4136 *fax* (0151) 478 4140
website www.nmgm.org.uk *e-mail* claire.rider@nmgm.org

Liverpool (Lady Lever)

The Lady Lever houses an impressive collection including tapestries and embroideries, pre-Raphaelite paintings, Wedgwood, 18th-century furniture, Napoleonic memorabilia and Roman sculpture. Please phone for full details of current exhibitions. Open 10:00–5:00 Monday–Saturday, 12:00–5:00 Sunday.

- ■ Not a Pretty Sight: Portraits that Sitters Hated — To Jan 02
- ➤ Leonardo Drawings from the Royal Collection* — 15 Feb – 21 Apr 02
  - ➤ *Lady Lever Art Gallery, Liverpool* ➤ *Swansea* ➤ *Graves Art Gallery, Sheffield*

Liverpool Museum, William Brown Street, Liverpool, L3 8EN
tel (0151) 478 4399
website www.nmgm.org.uk
Please phone or consult the website for full details of current exhibitions.

- ■ Horrible Histories: Funfair of Fear — To 6 Jan 02
- ■ The Earl and the Pussycat: Lord Derby's Life and Legacy* — 31 May – 29 Sept 02

Sudley House, Mosley Hill Road, Liverpool, L18 5BX
tel (0151) 724 3245
website www.nmgm.org.uk *e-mail* claire.rider@nmgm.org
A fine collection of 18th- and 19th-century paintings, furniture and decorative arts, including works by Gainsborough, Turner and the Pre-Raphaelite Brotherhood.

Tate Liverpool, Albert Dock, Liverpool, L3 4BB
tel (0151) 702 7400 *fax* (0151) 702 7401
website www.tate.org.uk *e-mail* liverpoolinfo@tate.org.uk

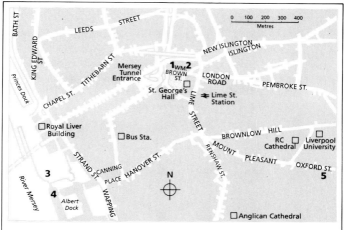

Liverpool

1 Lady Lever Art Gallery
2 Walker Art Gallery
3 Merseyside Maritime Museum
4 Tate Gallery
5 University of Liverpool Art Collections

Liverpool (Tate)

Tate Liverpool displays works from the Tate collection of modern art, alongside special exhibitions of internationally renowned contemporary artists. Please phone or consult the website for full details of current exhibitions. Open 10:00–5:00 Tuesday–Sunday (closed 1 January, Good Friday, and 24–26 December). Admission to the collection is free, but there are charges for entry to special exhibitions.

- Paul McCarthy* — To 13 Jan 02
  Originated by the New Museum of Contemporary Art, New York
- Emotional Ties — To 24 Feb 02
- Telling Tales — To Aug 02
- Modern British Art — To Dec 02
- Liverpool Biennial* — 14 Sept – 24 Nov 02
- Shopping* — 12 Dec 02 – Aug 03

University of Liverpool Art Gallery, 3 Abercromby Square, Liverpool, L69 7WY
tel (0151) 794 2348 *fax* (0151) 794 2343
e-mail acompton@liverpool.ac.uk
The University gallery displays include watercolours and paintings by Joseph Wright and J. M. W. Turner, paintings by J. J. Audubon, early English porcelain, stained-glass cartoons by Burne-Jones, portraits by Augustus John, sculpture by John Foley and Lord Leighton, and 20th-century works by Epstein, Lucian Freud and Elisabeth Frink. Please phone for full details of current exhibitions.

- People and Places: A Retrospective of Work by Evelyn Gibbs (1905–1991) — 14 Jan – 15 Mar 02

Walker Art Gallery, William Brown Street, Liverpool, L3 8EL
tel (0151) 478 4199
website www.nmgm.org.uk

Liverpool (Walker) > Llandudno

A major collection of works ranging from the 12th to the 20th century. Artists represented include Rembrandt, Turner, Constable and David Hockney. Please phone or consult the website for full details of current exhibitions.

- George Romney 1734–1802* — 8 Feb – 21 Apr 02
- The Art of Paul McCartney* — Spring – Summer 02
- John Moores 22: Exhibition of Contemporary Painting — Sept 02 – Spring 03

Llandudno

Llandudno Museum, 17–19 Gloddaeth Street, Llandudno, Conwy, LL30 2DD
tel/fax (01492) 876517
e-mail llandudno.museum@lineone.net
Permanent displays include the Chardon Collection of paintings, sculptures and *objets d'art*. Temporary exhibitions include contemporary art, crafts and local history themes. Please phone for full details. Opening hours are 10:30–1:00 and 2:00–5:00 Tuesday–Saturday and 2:15–5:00 Sunday, from Easter to 31 October; and 1:30–4:30 Tuesday–Saturday from 1 November to Easter.

Oriel Mostyn, 12 Vaughan Street, Llandudno, Conwy, LL30 1AB
tel (01492) 879201 *fax* (01492) 878869
website www.mostyn.org *e-mail* anders@mostyn.org
Please phone or consult the website for full details of current exhibitions.

- ➤ Out of Line: Drawings from the Arts Council Collection*
  NTE from the Hayward Gallery, London — To 26 Jan 02
- Craig Wood* — 2 Feb – 16 Mar 02
- Mostyn Open 12 — 23 Mar – 11 May 02

London

Agnew's, 43 Old Bond Street, London, W1S 4BA
tel (020) 7290 9250 *fax* (020) 7629 4359
website www.agnewsgallery.com
e-mail agnews@agnewsgallery.co.uk
Agnew's presents new exhibitions of contemporary work every month. Open 9:30–5:30 Monday to Friday, 11:00–4:00 Saturdays. Please phone for full details of current exhibitions.

Alan Cristea Gallery, 31 Cork Street, London, W1S 3NU
tel (020) 7439 1866 *fax* (020) 7734 1549
website www.alancristea.com *e-mail* info@alancristea.co.uk
The gallery publishes and deals in 20th-century original prints and holds an extensive collection of works by artists including Picasso, Matisse, Miro and Hodgkin. Prints exclusively published by the gallery include works by Lisa Milroy, Julian Opie, Catherine Yass and Langlands & Bell. Exhibitions for 2002 include new works by Ian McKeever and Mick Moon, a Joe Tilson print retrospective, and mixed theme shows of the best 20th-century prints. Please phone for full details.

Angela Flowers Gallery, Flowers East, 199–205 Richmond Road, London, E8 3NJ
tel (020) 8985 3333 *fax* (020) 8985 0067
website www.flowerseast.com *e-mail* gallery@flowerseast.com
One of the largest contemporary art galleries in Britain, Flowers East represents over thirty artists. Exhibitions change monthly, and there is a separate graphics gallery. Opening hours are 10:00–6:00 Tuesday–Saturday. Please phone or consult the website for full details of current exhibitions.

London (Annely Juda > Bankside)

Annely Juda Fine Art, 23 Dering Street, London, W1S 1AW
tel (020) 7629 7578 *fax* (020) 7491 2139
website www.annelyjudafineart.co.uk
Annely Juda Fine Art specialises in contemporary painting and sculpture, Russian Constructivists, Bauhaus and early 20th-century art. Please phone or consult the website for full details of current exhibitions.

Apsley House, Wellington Museum, Hyde Park Corner, London, W1J 7NT
tel (020) 7499 5676 *fax* (020) 7493 6576
website www.apsleyhouse.org.uk *e-mail* e.appleby@vam.ac.uk
Apsley House was bought by the Duke of Wellington in 1817 and today houses his magnificent collection of sculpture, silver, porcelain, furniture, medals, memorabilia, and paintings by artists such as Velazquez, Goya, Rubens, Teniers, Lawrence, Wilkie and various Dutch masters. The collection is largely arranged as it was by the first Duke.

Artaid Biennial, 73 Collier Street, London, N1 9BE
tel (0131) 667 0390 *fax* (0131) 466 0519
website www.crusaid.org.uk *e-mail* artaid@crusaid.org.uk
A large show to be held in October 2002, including some of the most distinguished and internationally acclaimed contemporary artists. All profit from the sales of works will go to Crusaid, the national fundraiser for HIV and AIDS. Please phone or e-mail for full details.

Bankside Gallery, 48 Hopton Street, London, SE1 9JH
tel (020) 7928 7521 *fax* (020) 7928 2820
e-mail bankside@freeuk.com

London (Bankside > Barbican)

- Season's Greetings — To 27 Jan 02
- Japan 2001: Contemporary Works of Art on Paper — 14 Feb – 10 Mar 02
- Royal Watercolour Society Spring Exhibition — 21 Mar – 28 Apr 02
- Royal Society of Painter-Printmakers Annual Exhibition — 15 May – 16 June 02
- Watercolour C21 — 10 – 28 July 02
- Mixed Show, Selling — 1 Aug – 1 Sept 02
- ➤ Capel-y-Ffin to Ditchling: Watercolours and Drawings by Edgar Holloway* — 3 – 22 Sept 02
    - ➤ *Ditchling Museum* ➤ *National Museum of Wales, Aberystwyth* ➤ *Brecknock Museum & Art Gallery, Brecon* ➤ *Tunbridge Wells Museum & Art Gallery* ➤ *Bankside Gallery*
- Royal Watercolour Society Autumn Exhibition — 27 Sept – 20 Oct 02
- June Berry VPRWS RE — 24 Oct – 17 Nov 02
- Christmas Show — 23 Nov 02 – Jan 03

Barbican Art Gallery, Barbican Centre, Level 3, Silk Street, London, EC2Y 8DS
tel (020) 7638 8891 *fax* (020) 7382 7241
website www.barbican.org.uk
e-mail info@barbican.org.uk
Open 10:00–6:00 Monday–Tuesday and Thursday–Saturday, 10:00–8:00 Wednesday, 12:00–6:00 Sunday. Disabled access.

- Transition: The London Art Scene in the Fifties — 31 Jan – 14 Apr 02
- Martin Parr — 31 Jan – 14 Apr 02
- California! — 1 Feb – 4 May 02
- Barbican: This was Tomorrow — 20 Feb – 7 Apr 02

London (Barbican > Bernard Jacobson)

➤ Game On 16 May – 15 Sept 02
  ➤ *Barbican Art Gallery, London* ➤ *Museum of Scotland* ➤ *Europe*
■ Dressing Down: Contemporary Art, 10 Oct 02 – 5 Jan 03
  Fashion and Photography

Ben Uri Gallery, The London Jewish Museum of Art,
The Manor House, 80 East End Road, London N3 2SY
tel (020) 8349 5724
website www.benuri.com *e-mail* BenUri@ort.org
The Ben Uri was founded in 1915 in Whitechapel, East London to give a platform for Jewish artists (often immigrant) to exhibit – and to build a collection of works by contemporary Jewish artists. As a result, the gallery houses the largest collection of Anglo-Jewish artists in the world – close to 1000 works by over 300 artists – with masterpieces by Bomberg, Gertler, Epstein, Kramer, Meninsky and many more. The gallery is open by appointment only unless showing an exhibition. Please note that the gallery is hoping to move in the near future so please refer to the website for full details.

Berkeley Square Gallery, 23a Bruton Street, London, W1J 6QG
tel (020) 7493 7939 *fax* (020) 7493 7798
website www.bsgart.com *e-mail* info@bsgart.com
The gallery's collection comprises 20th-century sculpture, paintings, drawings and prints by modern masters such as Henry Moore and Lynn Chadwick, and contemporary British painting, sculpture and ceramics. Please phone for full details of current exhibitions.

Bernard Jacobson Gallery, 14a Clifford Street, London, W1S 4JY
tel (020) 7495 8575 *fax* (020) 7495 6210
website www.jacobsongallery.com *e-mail* mail@jacobsongallery.com
The permanent collection includes work by such artists as Donald

Judd, Peter Lanyon, Ben Nicholson, Robert Rauschenberg, Graham Sutherland, Marc Vaux, Glynn Williams and Anthony Caro. Please phone or consult the website for full details of current exhibitions.

The British Library, 96 Euston Road, London, NW1 2DB
tel (020) 7412 7332 *fax* (020) 7412 7340
website www.bl.uk *e-mail* visitor-services@bl.uk
The British Library houses a permanent exhibition drawn from the Library's collections. Themes include illuminated manuscripts, the dawn of printing, and maps and views. Amongst other displays within the Library are the Art of the Book, in the Pearson Gallery, and the history of book production, in the Workshop of Words, Sound and Images. Please phone or consult the website for full details of current exhibitions.

The British Museum, Great Russell Street, London, WC1B 3DG
tel (020) 7323 8000 *fax* (020) 7323 8616
website www.thebritishmuseum.ac.uk
e-mail info@thebritishmuseum.ac.uk
The British Museum's collections are divided into nine departments: Ancient Near East, Coins and Medals, Egyptian antiquities, Ethnography, Greek and Roman antiquities, Medieval and Modern Europe, Oriental antiquities, Prints and Drawings, and Prehistory and early Europe.

- ■ Light Motifs: An Aomori Float and Japanese Kites — To 3 Mar 02
- ➤ Agatha Christie and Archaeology: Mystery in Mesopotamia* — To 24 Mar 02
    ➢ *Ruhrland Museum, Essen* ➢ *Berlin* ➢ *British Museum, London*
- ■ Unknown Amazon: Nature in Culture in Ancient Brazil* — To 1 Apr 02

London (British Museum > Browse & Darby)

- ■ Japanese Prints from the Occupation — 17 Jan – 19 May 02
- ➤ Imaging Ulysses: Richard Hamilton's Illustrations to James Joyce* — 31 Jan – 19 May 02
  - ➤ *British Museum, London* ➤ *Irish Museum of Modern Art, Dublin*
- ■ The Hunt for Paradise: Court Arts of Safavid Iran 1501–1576* — 17 May – 15 Sept 02
- ■ The Queen of Sheba: Treasures from the Yemen* — 7 June – 13 Oct 02
- ■ From Breughel to Rembrandt: The George Abrams Collection of Dutch and Flemish Drawings — 13 June – 22 Sept 02
- ➤ Antony Gormley's 'Field for the British Isles' — 15 Nov 02 – 12 Jan 03
  NTE from the Hayward Gallery, London

Brixton Art Gallery, 35 Station Road, Brixton, London, SW9 8PB
tel/fax (020) 7733 6957
website www.brixtonartgallery.co.uk
e-mail brixart@brixtonartgallery.co.uk
Please phone or consult the website for full details of current exhibitions.

Browse & Darby, 19 Cork Street, London, W1X 2LP
tel (020) 7734 7984 *fax* (020) 7851 6650
website www.browseanddarby.co.uk
e-mail art@browseanddarby.co.uk
Dealers in 19th- and 20th-century French and British paintings, drawings and sculpture, plus contemporary British artists.
Please phone or consult the website for full details of current exhibitions.

London (Bruton Street > Canada House)

The Bruton Street Gallery, 28 Bruton Street,
London, W1X 7DB
tel (020) 7499 9747 *fax* (020) 7409 7867
website www.brutonstreetgallery.com
e-mail art@brutonstreetgallery.com
The Bruton Street Gallery offers a monthly programme of exhibitions of contemporary painting and sculpture by new as well as established gallery artists and sculptors such as William Foreman, Simon Gales, Vayreda C., David Backhouse, Stephen Broadbent and Ian Carrick amongst others. Please phone or consult the website for full details of current exhibitions.

Camden Arts Centre, Arkwright Road, London, NW3 6DG
tel (020) 7435 2643 *fax* (020) 7794 3371
website www.camdenartscentre.org
e-mail info@camdenartscentre.org
Please phone or consult the website for full details of current exhibitions.

- Roman Signer*　　　　　　　　　　To 3 Feb 02
- Douglas Huebler　　　　　　　　　15 Feb – 14 Apr 02
- David Shrigley　　　　　　　　　　15 Feb – 14 Apr 02

Canada House Gallery, Canada House, Trafalgar Square,
London, SW1
tel (020) 7258 6366/6537 *fax* (020) 7258 6434
website www.dfait-maeci.gc.ca/london
e-mail michael.regan@dfait-maeci.gc.ca
A rotating collection of Inuit earrings and felt pictures, plus prints and drawings relating to the architecture and interior decoration of the gallery building. Please phone or consult the website for full details of current exhibitions.

London (Canada House > Church Farmhouse)

- ■ Larry Towell: Photographic Portrait of the Canadian Mennonite Communities*
  Originated by Magnum Photo-Agency
  To Feb 02
- ■ Contemporary Inuit Carvings and Printmaking*
  May – July 02

The Catto Gallery, 100 Heath Street, London, NW3 1DP
tel (020) 7435 6660 *fax* (020) 7431 5620
website www.catto.co.uk *e-mail* art@catto.co.uk
Please phone or consult the website for full details of current exhibitions.

CCA Galleries (London), 517–523 Fulham Road, London, SW6 1HD
tel (020) 7386 4900 *fax* (020) 7386 4919
website www.ccagalleries.com *e-mail* gallery@ccagalleries.com
CCA Galleries (London) house contemporary prints, ceramics and original works by a variety of artists, including Heidi König, Richard Tuff, Annora Spence, Umaña-Clarke and Katty McMurray. Please phone or consult the website for full details of current exhibitions.

Church Farmhouse Museum, Greyhound Hill, Hendon, London, NW4 4JR
tel (020) 8203 0130 *fax* (020) 8359 2666
website www.earl.org.uk/partners/barnet/churchf.htm
The museum occupies a building of mid-17th century origin with Victorian additions. It has three reconstructed 19th-century furnished rooms on the ground floor, while the first floor houses a continuous programme of temporary exhibitions. Please phone for full details.

- ■ J. F. Horrabin: Cartoonist, Cartographer and Socialist
  Spring 02
- ■ British Toys and Games
  Dec 02 – Feb 03

London (Colnaghi > Courtauld)

Colnaghi Gallery, 15 Old Bond Street, London, W1X 4JL
tel (020) 7491 7408 *fax* (020) 7491 8851
website www.colnaghi.co.uk *e-mail* ukcolnaghi@aol.com
The gallery's permanent collection comprises Master paintings and drawings of the period 1500–1900. Please phone or consult the website for full details of current exhibitions.

Commonwealth Institute, Kensington High Street, London, W8 6NQ
tel (020) 7603 4535 *fax* (020) 7602 7374
website www.commonwealth.org.uk
The main gallery will be closed throughout the year for refurbishment, but in March a new space will be opening with a programme of exhibitions featuring contemporary art from Commonwealth artists, complemented by ethnographic displays with accompanying workshops and events. Please see the website for updates.

Courtauld Gallery, Courtauld Institute of Art, Somerset House, Strand, London, WC2R 0RN
tel (020) 7848 2526 *fax* (020) 7848 2589
website www.courtauld.ac.uk
e-mail galleryinfo@courtauld.ac.uk
The gallery houses an important collection of European paintings from the 14th century to the 20th, including one of the finest collections of Impressionist and Post-Impressionist paintings in the world. Please phone for full details of current exhibitions.

- Art on the Line: The Royal Academy Exhibitions at Somerset House 1780–1836* To 20 Jan 02
- Drawn to Painting: Kossoff after Poussin Feb – May 02
- Sculptures by Lipchitz June – Sept 02
- Van Dyck and Titian* Aug – Oct 02

London (Crafts Council > Dulwich)

Crafts Council, 44a Pentonville Road, Islington, London, N1 9BY
tel (020) 7278 7700 *fax* (020) 7837 6891
website www.craftscouncil.org.uk
The Crafts Council's collection of contemporary crafts is a unique resource which is offered on loan to organisations engaged in public exhibitions and education. Please phone or consult the website for full details of current exhibitions.

Design Museum, 28 Shad Thames, London, SE1 2YD
tel (020) 7403 6933, *fax* (020) 7378 6540
website www.designmuseum.org
e-mail enquiries@design-museum.org.uk
The Design Museum's collection illustrates the development of design in mass production, explaining how design affects daily life and why consumer products work and look the way they do, as well as showcasing the best of contemporary designs and technologies. Open 10:00–5:45 daily. Please phone or consult the website for full details of current exhibitions.

- Conran Foundation Collection: Marc Newson — To Feb 02
- Saul Bass — To Mar 02
- John Galliano at Christian Dior — To 28 Apr 02

Dulwich Picture Gallery, College Road, London, SE21 7AD
tel (020) 8693 5254 *fax* (020) 8299 8700
website www.dulwichpicturegallery.org.uk
e-mail k.knowles@dulwichpicturegallery.org.uk
Dating back to 1811, the Dulwich is England's oldest public art gallery. Its collection includes works by Poussin, Claude, Rubens, Van Dyck, Teniers, Murillo, Rembrandt, Hobbema, Lely, Hogarth, Gainsborough, Reynolds, Watteau, Tiepolo and Canaletto.

London (Dulwich > Fine Art Society)

- William Beckford* 6 Feb – 14 Apr 02
- Inspired by Italy: Dutch Landscape Painters 1600–1700* 22 May – 26 Aug 02
- David Wilkie* 11 Sept – 1 Dec 02

Estorick Collection of Modern Italian Art, 39a Canonbury Square, London, N1 2AN
tel (020) 7704 9522 *fax* (020) 7704 9531
website www.estorickcollection.com
e-mail curator@estorickcollection.com
Paintings and drawings by Italian figurative artists of the first half of the 20th century form the core of the collection, including works by Futurists Balla, Boccioni, Carrà, Russolo and Severini, the great metaphysical painter Giorgio de Chirico, Giorgio Morandi and Modigliani, among others. Please phone for full details of current exhibitions.

- Carlo Carrà: Works on Paper* To 20 Jan 02
- Boyd Webb 1 May – 9 June 02
- ➤ Under Mussolini: Decorated Propaganda Art in the 1920s and 1930s 2 Oct – 22 Dec 02
  In collaboration with the Wolfsonian Foundation, Genoa

The Fine Art Society, 148 New Bond Street, London, W1S 2JT
tel (020) 7629 5116 *fax* (020) 7491 9451
website www.the-fine-art-society.co.uk *e-mail* faslondon@aol.com
Founded in 1876, the Fine Art Society specialises in 19th- and 20th-century paintings, sculpture, furniture and decorative arts, including the work of James McNeill Whistler, Charles Rennie Mackintosh, the Scottish Colourists, and furniture of the Arts and Crafts Movement. Please phone or consult the website for full details.

London (Geffrye Museum > Gimpel Fils)

Geffrye Museum, Kingsland Road, London, E2 8EA
tel (020) 7739 9893 *fax* (020) 7729 5647
website www.geffrye-museum.org.uk
e-mail info@geffrye-museum.org.uk

The Geffrye is the only museum in Britain to specialise in the domestic interiors of the urban middle-classes. Its displays form a sequence of period rooms which range from 1600 to the present day, complemented during the summer months by a series of historical garden rooms covering the same period.

- ■ Christmas Past: Seasonal Traditions in English Homes* — To 6 Jan 02
- ■ After the Fire: London Furniture 1066–1714 — To 3 Mar 02
- ➤ Cutting Edge: A History of British Cutlery and Place Settings* — 26 Mar – 2 June 02
  - ➤ *Fairfax House, York* ➤ *Millennium Galleries, Sheffield* ➤ *Geffrye Museum, London*
- ➤ Onetree* — 25 June – Sept 02
  - ➤ *Royal Botanic Gardens, Edinburgh* ➤ *Harley Gallery, Nottinghamshire* ➤ *Tatten Park, Cheshire* ➤ *Bristol Museum & Art Gallery* ➤ *Geffrye Museum, London*
- ■ Christmas Past: Seasonal Traditions in English Homes* — Dec 02

Gimpel Fils Limited, 30 Davies Street, London, W1K 4NB
tel/fax (020) 7493 2488
website www.gimpelfils.com
e-mail info@gimpelfils.com

Please phone or consult the website for full details of current exhibitions.

London (Hampstead Museum > The Hayward)

Hampstead Museum, Burgh House, New End Square, London, NW3 1LT
tel (020) 7431 0144 *fax* (020) 7435 8817
e-mail hampsteadmuseum@talk21.com
The first floor contains the museum, while the first-floor art gallery houses a changing programme of two- to three-week exhibitions featuring the work of local artists, sculptors and potters. The Museum is closed on Mondays and Tuesdays. Please phone for full details.

The Hayward Gallery, Belvedere Road, London, SE1 8XZ
tel (020) 7928 3144 *fax* (020) 7401 2664
website www.haywardgallery.org.uk
e-mail visual_arts@hayward.org.uk
A purpose-built modern art gallery which presents a wide range of groundbreaking exhibitions. Open 10:00–6:00 Thursday–Monday, 10:00–8:00 Tuesday–Wednesday. Please phone or consult the website for full details of current exhibitions.

- Paul Klee*   17 Jan – 1 Apr 02
- Ann-Sofi Sidén*   17 Jan – 1 Apr 02
- Ansel Adams*   July – Sep 02
- Douglas Gordon*   Oct 02 – Jan 03

The Hayward Gallery manages the Arts Council Collection on behalf of the Arts Council of England. The Collection is not normally displayed at the Hayward, which instead arranges touring exhibitions. In addition, many individual works are on view in galleries and public places throughout the UK.

National Touring Exhibitions (NTE)
- ➤ Spotlight on Antony Gormley: Field for the British Isles   To 12 Jan 03

London (The Hayward)

- ➤ *British Museum, London* ➤ *Tullie House Museum & Gallery, Carlisle*
- ▶ At Home With Art* To 5 May 02
  - ➤ *The Manx Museum, Douglas* ➤ *Bowes Museum, Barnard Castle* ➤ *Duff House, Banff*
- ▶ David Hockney: Grimm's Fairy Tales To 8 Sept 02
  - ➤ *Ards Arts Centre, Newtownards* ➤ *The Black Swan Guild, Frome* ➤ *Wednesbury Museum & Art Gallery* ➤ *Luton Museum & Art Gallery* ➤ *Alfred East Art Gallery, Kettering* ➤ *Wingfield Arts*
- ▶ Out of Line: Drawings from the Arts Council Collection To 20 Oct 02
  - ➤ *Oriel Mostyn, Llandudno* ➤ *The Potteries Museum & Art Gallery, Stoke-on-Trent* ➤ *Middlesbrough Art Gallery* ➤ *Wingfield Arts* ➤ *Burton Art Gallery, Bideford*
- ▶ Bridget Riley: Silkscreen Prints and Gouaches 1963–2001 To 22 Dec 02
  - ➤ *Ferens Art Gallery, Kingston upon Hull* ➤ *Hunterian Art Gallery, Glasgow* ➤ *Abbot Hall Art Gallery, Kendal*
- ▶ Fleeting Arcadias: Thirty Years of British Landscape Photography from the Arts Council Collection 10 Jan – 8 Sept 02
  - ➤ *Ucheldre Centre, Holyhead* ➤ *Burstow Gallery, Brighton* ➤ *St Barbe Museum, Lymington* ➤ *North Berwick Museum, Haddington* ➤ *Spout Farmhouse, Telford*
- ▶ Followers of Fashion: Graphic Satires from the Georgian Period 12 Jan – 10 Mar 02
  - ➤ *Hatton Gallery, Newcastle upon Tyne*
- ▶ Spotlight on Kenneth Martin 12 Jan – 20 July 02
  - ➤ *Peter Scott Gallery, Lancaster* ➤ *Rhyl Library, Museum & Art Gallery* ➤ *Denbigh & Buckley Libraries* ➤ *Huddersfield Art Gallery*

London (The Hayward > Hazlitt, Gooden & Fox)

- Picasso: Histoire Naturelle 12 Jan – Jan 03
  - *McLean Museum & Art Gallery, Greenock* > *Chatelherault, Ferniegar* > *Oakham Theatre* > *Eastleigh Museum* > *Washington Arts Centre* > *Falmouth Art Gallery*
- Dubuffet's Walls: Lithographs for 'Les Murs' 26 Jan – 24 Feb 02
  - *Herne Bay Museum*
- Trauma 26 Jan – 17 Apr 02
  - *Museum of Modern Art, Oxford*
- Matisse: Jazz from the Arts Council Collection 26 Jan – 27 Oct 02
  - *The Ropewalk, Barton-on-Humber* > *Thelma Hulbert Gallery, Honiton* > *Yale College, Wrexham* > *Riverhouse Barn, Walton on Thames* > *St Barbe Museum, Lymington* > *North Berwick Museum, Haddington* > *Oakham Theatre*
- Käthe Kollwitz: Artist of the People 14 Feb – 21 Apr 02
  - *Abbot Hall Art Gallery, Kendal*
- Edward Weston 16 Feb – 17 Mar 02
  - *Beldam Gallery, Uxbridge*
- Goya: The Disparates 6 Apr – 5 May 02
  - *Bedales Gallery, Petersfield*
- Printers Inc: Recent British Prints 1 – 30 June 02
  - *Whitstable Museum & Art Gallery*

Hazlitt, Gooden & Fox Ltd, 38 Bury Street, St James's, London, SW1Y 6BB
tel (020) 7930 6422 *fax* (020) 7839 5984
e-mail info@hazlittgoodenand fox.com
The Hazlitt, Gooden & Fox specialise in Old Master paintings and drawings and 19th-century French drawings.

London (Hermitage Rooms > Iveagh Bequest)

Hermitage Rooms at Somerset House, South Building, Somerset House, Strand, London, WC2R 1LA
tel (020) 7845 4631 *fax* (020) 7845 4637
website www.hermitagerooms.com
Opening hours are 10:00–6:00 daily (but 12:00–6:00 on 1 January). There is wheelchair access to all galleries. Please phone for full details of current exhibitions.

- French Drawings and Paintings from the Hermitage: Poussin to Picasso*   To 3 Mar 02

ICA Gallery, The Mall, London, SW1Y 5AH
tel (020) 7930 3647 *fax* (020) 7873 0051
website www.ica.org.uk *e-mail* info@ica.org.uk
Open 12:00–7:30 daily. Limited wheelchair access. Please phone or consult the website for full details of current exhibitions.

- Francois Roche, Pierre Huygue, Phillipa Pareno, MM Design   To 13 Jan 02

Imperial War Museum, Lambeth Road, London, SE1 6HZ
tel (020) 7416 5320 *fax* (020) 7416 5374
website www.iwm.org.uk *e-mail* vmain@iwm.org.uk
The IWM's collections are enormous and encompass a wealth of objects, works of art, documents, film, photographs, books, maps and sound recordings. The collections have been built up around the two World Wars and conflicts since 1945. Please phone for full details of current exhibitions.

Iveagh Bequest, Kenwood House, Hampstead Lane, London, NW3 7JP
tel (020) 8348 1286 *fax* (020) 7973 3891
website www.english-heritage.org.uk

London (Iveagh Bequest > Lisson)

The Iveagh Bequest includes work by Rembrandt, Vermeer, Turner, Reynolds, Gainsborough, Van Dyck and Frans Hals. Admission to Kenwood House is free. Please phone or consult the website for full details of current exhibitions.

- ■ Clerics and Connoisseurs: An Irish Collection through the Centuries* To 27 Jan 02

The Jewish Museum, Finchley, The Sternberg Centre, 80 East End Road, London, N3 2SY
tel (020) 8349 1143 *fax* (020) 8343 2162
website www.jewmusm.ort.org *e-mail* jml.finchley@lincone.net
The museum's social history collection includes an oral history archive, a photographic archive (with over 15,000 images) and a wide range of documents and artefacts reflecting the diverse roots and heritage of Jews in Britain.

- ■ Am I my Brother's Keeper? Rescue in the Holocaust Jan – Apr 02
- ■ Jewish London: Photographs from the Archives* May – Oct 02

Lefevre Gallery, 30 Bruton Street, London, W1X
tel (020) 7493 2107 *fax* (020) 7499 9088
website www.lefevre-gallery.com
e-mail contemporary@lefevre-gallery.co.uk
The gallery's permanent collection comprises Impressionist, post Impressionist, 20th-century and contemporary works of art. Please phone or consult the website for full details of current exhibitions.

Lisson Gallery, 52–54 Bell Street, London, NW1 5DA
tel (020) 7724 2736 *fax* (020) 7724 7124
Please phone for full details of current exhibitions.

London Map 1

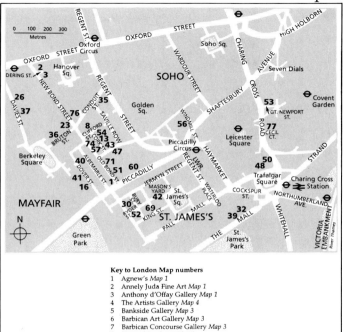

Key to London Map numbers
1. Agnew's *Map 1*
2. Annely Juda Fine Art *Map 1*
3. Anthony d'Offay Gallery *Map 1*
4. The Artists Gallery *Map 4*
5. Bankside Gallery *Map 3*
6. Barbican Art Gallery *Map 3*
7. Barbican Concourse Gallery *Map 3*
8. Bernard Jacobson *Map 1*
9. Bethnal Green Museum of Childhood *off Map 3*
10. British Architectural Library Drawings *Map 2*
11. The British Library *Map 3*
12. The British Museum *Map 3*
13. Browse & Darby *Map 1*
14. Camden Arts Centre *Map 4*
15. The Cartoon Art Trust *Map 3*
16. CCA Galleries *Map 1*
17. Church Farmhouse Museum *Map 4*
18. The Commonwealth Experience *off Map 2*
19. Courtauld Gallery *Map 3*
20. Crafts Council Gallery *Map 3*
21. Design Museum *Map 3*

London Map 2

22 Dulwich Picture Gallery *off Map 3*
23 Fine Art Society Ltd. *Map 1*
24 Flowers East *off Map 3*
25 Geffrye Museum *off Map 3*
26 Gimpel Fils *Map 1*
27 Goethe Institut *Map 2*
28 Hampstead Museum *Map 4*
29 The Hayward Gallery *Map 3*
30 Hazlitt, Gooden & Fox Ltd. *Map 1*
31 Imperial War Museum *Map 3*
32 Institute of Contemporary Arts *Map 1*
33 Iveagh Bequest *Map 4*
34 Jack Duncan Cartoons and Books *Map 3*
35 Jason & Rhodes *Map 1*
36 Lefevre Gallery *Map 1*
37 The London Institute *Map 1*
38 The London Museum of Jewish Life *Map 4*
39 Mall Galleries *Map 1*
40 Marlborough Fine Art (London) Ltd. *Map 1*
41 Marlborough Graphics Ltd. *Map 1*
42 Matthiesen Fine Arts *Map 1*

London Map 3

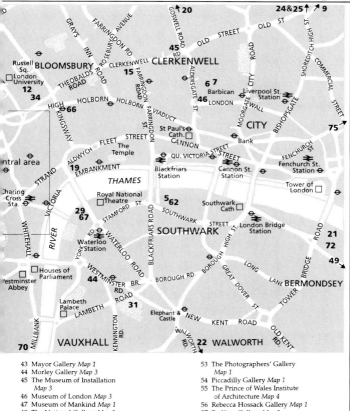

43 Mayor Gallery *Map 1*
44 Morley Gallery *Map 3*
45 The Museum of Installation *Map 3*
46 Museum of London *Map 3*
47 Museum of Mankind *Map 1*
48 The National Gallery *Map 1*
49 National Maritime Museum *off Map 3*
50 National Portrait Gallery *Map 1*
51 P. & D. Colnaghi & Co Ltd. *Map 1*
52 Peter Nahum *Map 1*

53 The Photographers' Gallery *Map 1*
54 Piccadilly Gallery *Map 1*
55 The Prince of Wales Institute of Architecture *Map 4*
56 Rebecca Hossack Gallery *Map 1*
57 Redfern Gallery *Map 1*
58 RIBA Architecture Centre *Map 2*
59 RIBA Heinz Gallery *Map 2*
60 Royal Academy of Arts *Map 1*
61 Royal College of Arts Galleries *Map 2*

London Map 4

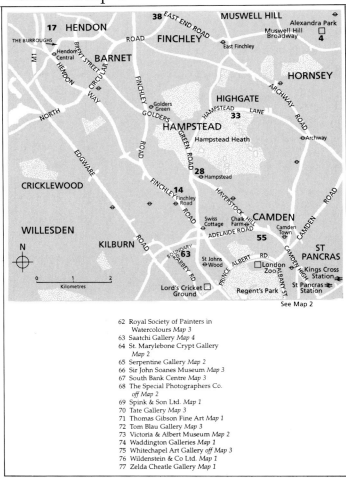

62 Royal Society of Painters in Watercolours *Map 3*
63 Saatchi Gallery *Map 4*
64 St. Marylebone Crypt Gallery *Map 2*
65 Serpentine Gallery *Map 2*
66 Sir John Soanes Museum *Map 3*
67 South Bank Centre *Map 3*
68 The Special Photographers Co. *off Map 2*
69 Spink & Son Ltd. *Map 1*
70 Tate Gallery *Map 3*
71 Thomas Gibson Fine Art *Map 1*
72 Tom Blau Gallery *Map 3*
73 Victoria & Albert Museum *Map 2*
74 Waddington Galleries *Map 1*
75 Whitechapel Art Gallery *off Map 3*
76 Wildenstein & Co Ltd. *Map 1*
77 Zelda Cheatle Gallery *Map 1*

London (Institute > Marlborough)

The London Institute Gallery, 65 Davies Street, London, W1K 5DA
tel (020) 7514 8083 *fax* (020) 7514 6131
website www.linst.ac.uk *e-mail* gallery@linst.ac.uk
Please phone or consult website for full details of current exhibitions.

- ➤ Manga: Short Comics from Modern Japan* 9 Jan – 8 Feb 02
  Originated by The Japan Foundation
- ■ Zero–Hans Schleger: A Life of Design* 15 Feb – 14 Mar 02
- ■ Young at Art: Awards for Young Artists in London* 21 Mar – 19 Apr 02
- ■ (X)hibit: London Institute Students' Union Show* 1 May – 13 June 02
- ■ 100 Posters: The Odermatt Collection* 26 June – 22 Aug 02

The Mall Galleries, The Mall, London, SW1Y 5BD
tel (020) 7930 6844 *fax* (020) 7839 7830
website www.mallgalleries.org.uk
e-mail vnewlandsmallgalleries@pop.dial.pipex.co.uk
The Mall Galleries host nine annual society exhibitions, as well as shows by non-society artists, featuring a varied array of contemporary art. Please phone or consult the website for full details of current exhibitions.

Marlborough Fine Art (London) Ltd, 6 Albemarle Street, London, W1S 4BY
tel (020) 7629 5161 *fax* (020) 7629 6338
website www.marlboroughfineart.com
e-mail mfa@marlboroughfineart.com
Marlborough Fine Art specialises in contemporary art and modern British artists. Gallery artists include Frank Auerbach, Lynn

London (Marlborough > Morley Gallery)

Chadwick, Stephen Conroy, Christopher Couch, Maggi Hambling, R. B. Kitaj, Sarah Raphael, Paula Rego, and the estates of Oscar Kokoschka, Victor Pasmore and Graham Sutherland. Please phone for full details of current exhibitions.

Matthiesen Fine Arts Ltd, 7 Masons Yard, Duke Street, St James, London, SW1Y 6BU
tel (020) 7930 2437 *fax* (020) 7930 1387
website www.europeanpaintings.com
e-mail matthiesen@oldmasterslondon.demon.co.uk
The gallery's permanent collection concentrates on Italian and French Old Masters of the period 1300–1800 and 19th-century French paintings. Please phone or consult the website for full details of current exhibitions.

The Mayor Gallery, 22a Cork Street, London, W1X 1HB
tel (020) 7734 3558 *fax* (020) 7494 1377
website www.artnet.com/mayor.htlm
e-mail mail@mayorgallery.com
The Mayor Gallery is London's leading dealer in Dada, Surrealism and Pop Art. Please phone or consult the website for full details of current exhibitions.

Morley Gallery, 61 Westminster Bridge Road, London, SE1 7HT
tel (020) 7450 9226 *fax* (020) 7928 4074
website www.morleycollege.ac.uk/gallery
e-mail gallery@morleycollege.ac.uk
Opening hours are 11:00–6:00 Monday–Wednesday and Friday, 11:00–7:00 Thursday, 12:00–4:00 Saturday. Closed Bank Holidays. Please phone or consult the website for full details of current exhibitions.

London (Morley Gallery > National Gallery)

- London International Small Print Biennale 2001/2002 — 7 – 17 Jan 02
- Chris Crooke — 7 – 28 Feb 02
- Crossing the Border — 7 Mar – 11 Apr 02
- Made @ Morley 2002: Morley Art Department Exhibition — 24 Apr – 16 May 02
- Morley College Art & Design and Textile Foundation End of Year Exhibition — 24 May – 6 June 02
- Derek Mawudoku — 12 – 27 June 02
- New Fibre Art — 4 – 19 July 02

The Museum of London, 150 London Wall, London, EC2Y 5HN
tel (020) 7600 3699 *fax* (020) 7600 1058
website www.museumoflondon.org.uk
e-mail jholmes@museumoflondon.org.uk
Collections cover every aspect of social life from prehistoric times to the present, through material ranging from archaeological finds to photographs and safety pins to shop fronts. The permanent galleries tell the story of London, while temporary exhibitions focus on particular topics or contemporary issues. Please phone or consult the website for full details of current exhibitions.

The National Gallery, Trafalgar Square, London, WC2N 5DN
tel (020) 7747 2885 *fax* (020) 7747 2423
website www.nationalgallery.org.uk
e-mail information@ng-london.org.uk
The National Gallery collection of European painting covers the period 1250–1900. It includes works by Van Eyck, Piero Della Francesca, Botticelli, Leonardo da Vinci, Raphael, Michelangelo, Holbein, Titian, El Greco, Rubens, Van Dyck, Poussin, Claude,

London (National Gallery > National Maritime)

Velazquez, Rembrandt, Vermeer, Gainsborough, Turner, Constable, Monet, Renoir, Cézanne, Van Gogh and Seurat.

- ■ Pisanello: Painter to the Renaissance Court* — To 13 Jan 02
- ■ Kitaj: In the Aura of Cézanne and Other Masters* — To 10 Feb 02
- ■ Goya: The Family of the Infante Don Luis* — To 3 Mar 02
- ➤ Aelbert Cuyp* — 13 Feb – 12 May 02
    - ➤ *National Gallery of Art, Washington* ➤ *National Gallery, London* ➤ *Rijksmuseum, Amsterdam*
- ■ Baroque Painting in Genoa — 13 Mar – 16 June 02
- ■ Fabric of Vision: Dress and Drapery in Painting — 19 June – 8 Sept 02
- ➤ Madame de Pompadour: Images of a Mistress — 16 Oct 02 – 12 Jan 03
    - ➤ *Château de Versailles* ➤ *Kunsthalle, Munich* ➤ *National Gallery, London*

National Maritime Museum, Greenwich, London, SE10 9NF
tel (020) 8858 4422 *fax* (020) 8312 6632
website www.nmm.ac.uk

The museum's collection of some two million items includes 4000 oil paintings tracing the history of Britain and the sea, while its collection of portraits is second only to London's National Portrait Gallery. Please phone or consult the website for full details of current exhibitions.

- ■ A Sea of Faces: Naval Portraiture 1600–2000 — Till June 02
- ■ Historic Greenwich — Throughout 02

London (National Portrait > New Academy)

National Portrait Gallery, St Martin's Place, London, WC2H 0HE
tel (020) 7306 0055 *fax* (020) 7306 0058
website www.npg.org.uk

The National Portrait Gallery is home to the largest collection of portraiture in the world. Over one thousand portraits are on display across three floors, with sitters ranging from Shakespeare to *The Rolling Stones*.

- ➤ Mirror Mirror: Self-Portraits by Women Artists* To 24 Feb 02
  - ➤ *National Portrait Gallery, London* ➤ *City Art Gallery, Leeds* ➤ *Victoria Art Gallery, Bath*
- ■ Mario Testino: Portraits* 2 Feb – 2 June 02
- ➤ Saving Faces: Portraits by Mark Gilbert 27 Feb – 21 Apr 02
  - ➤ *National Portrait Gallery, London* ➤ *City Art Gallery, Leeds* ➤ *Royal Albert Memorial Museum, Exeter*
- ■ Beatrix Potter to Harry Potter: Children's Writers in the 20th Century* 15 May – end Aug 02
- ■ George Romney (1734–1802)* 30 May – 18 Aug 02
- ■ BP Portrait Award 2002* 20 June – Sept 02
- ■ John Kobal Photographic Portrait Award 2002* Sept 02
- ■ Americans: Portraits from the National Portrait Gallery, Washington DC* Oct 02 – 12 Jan 03
- ■ Byronism* Nov 02 – Feb 03

The New Academy Gallery, 34 Windmill Street, Fitzrovia, London, W1T 2JR
tel (020) 7323 4700 *fax* (020) 7436 3059
website www.newacademygallery.com
e-mail gallery@curwengallery.com

London (New Academy > Photographers')

The gallery houses paintings, sculpture and original prints by contemporary British artists and Modern Masters. Please phone or consult the website for full details of current exhibitions.

198 Gallery, 198 Railton Road, London, SE24 0LU
tel (020) 7978 8309 *fax* (020) 7652 1418
website www.198gallery.co.uk *e-mail* gallery@198gallery.co.uk
The 198 Gallery presents exhibitions of contemporary art by artists from diverse cultural backgrounds working with a variety of media and issues within a multicultural context. Open 11:00–5:00 Monday–Friday, 12:00–4:00 Saturday.

- Eduardo Padhila — Mar – Apr 02
- Carlos Madriz — May – June 02
- Urban Vision: Project Exhibition — July 02

Percival David Foundation of Chinese Art, School of Oriental and African Studies, 53 Gordon Square, London, WC1H 0PD
tel (020) 7387 3909 *fax* (020) 7387 5163
e-mail sp17@soas.ac.uk
The Percival David Foundation of Chinese Art houses arguably the finest collection of Chinese ceramics outside China and a library of East Asian and Western books relating to Chinese art and culture. Please phone for full details of current exhibitions.

The Photographers' Gallery, 5 & 8 Great Newport Street, London, WC2H 7HY
tel (020) 7831 1772 *fax* (020) 7836 9704
website www.photonet.org.uk *e-mail* info@photonet.org.uk
Please phone or consult website for full details of current exhibitions.

- Re:mote — To 19 Jan 02

London (Photographers' > Redfern)

- The Citibank Private Bank Photography Prize 2002* 1 Feb – 23 Mar 02
- Brixton Archives Apr – May 02

Pump House Gallery, Battersea Park, London, SW11 4NJ
tel (020) 7350 0523 *fax* (020) 7228 9062
website www.wandsworth.gov.uk/gallery
e-mail pump-house@lineone.net
The Pump House runs a programme of temporary contemporary art exhibitions. Open Wednesday–Sunday all year round. Admission free. Please phone or consult website for full details of current exhibitions.

Rangers' House, Chesterfield Walk, Blackheath, London, SE10
tel (020) 8853 0035
Houses a permanent collection of primarily European fine and decorative art, including jewellery, paintings, sculpture, furniture, tapestries, enamels and ivories. Open from 10:00 Wednesday–Sunday and Bank Holidays, from Spring 2002 on.
- The Wernher Collection Spring 02

Rebecca Hossack Gallery, 35 Windmill Street, Fitzrovia, London, W1T 2JS
tel (020) 7436 4899 *fax* (020) 7323 3182
website www.r-h-g.co.uk *e-mail* rebecca@r-h-g.co.uk
Please phone or consult the website for full details of current exhibitions.

Redfern Gallery, 20 Cork Street, London, W1S 3HL
tel (020) 7734 1732 *fax* (020) 7494 2908
website www.redfern-gallery.com

London (Redfern > Royal College of Art)

e-mail art@redfern-gallery.com
The gallery deals in modern British, 20th-century European and contemporary art. Its policy since its foundation in 1923 has always been to promote the work of younger artists. Please phone or consult the website for full details of current exhibitions.

Royal Academy of Arts, Burlington House, Piccadilly, London, W1J 0BD
tel (020) 7300 8000 *fax* (020) 7300 8001
website www.royalacademy.org.uk
The Academy's permanent collections consist of British paintings and sculpture from the 18th to 20th centuries, including works by Reynolds, Turner, Constable, Millais, Spencer and Ayres. The RA is wheelchair accessible. Open 10:00–6:00 Saturday–Thursday, 10:00–10:00 Friday. Please phone or consult the website for full details of current exhibitions.

- The Dawn of the Floating World 1650–1765: Early Ukiyo-e Prints and Paintings* To 17 Feb 02
- Paris: Capital of the Arts 1900–1968* 26 Jan – 19 Apr 02
- Summer Exhibition 2002* 11 June – 19 Aug 02
- The Aztecs* 27 Sept 02 – 16 Feb 03

Royal College of Art Galleries, Kensington Gate, London, SW7 2EU
tel (020) 7590 4444 *fax* (020) 7590 4124
website www.rca.ac.uk *e-mail* k.williams@rca.ac.uk
The College has a complex of galleries hosting exhibitions of students' work, culminating in the internationally renowned summer show. The galleries also house various high profile public exhibitions of art, design and communications. Please phone or consult the website for full details of current exhibitions.

Royal Institute of British Architects, 66 Portland Place, London, W1B 1AD
tel (020) 7580 5533 *fax* (020) 7637 5775
website www.architecture.com
e-mail bal@inst.riba.org
Please phone or consult the website for full details of current exhibitions. Note that the Architectural Library Drawings Collection is presently closed to the public pending its transfer to the Victoria & Albert Museum in 2004.

- ■ Coming Homes: The Future of Mass Housing in the UK   Sept – Nov 02

Saatchi Gallery, 98a Boundary Road, London, NW8 0RH
tel (020) 7624 8299 *fax* (020) 7624 3798
The gallery draws from a collection of over two thousand paintings, sculptures and installations. Its aim is to introduce new or largely unseen art to a wider audience. Please phone for full details of current exhibitions. Open 12:00–6:00 Thursday–Sunday.

Scolar Fine Art, 35 Bruton Place, London, W1J 6NS
tel (020) 7629 4944 *fax* (020) 7629 4494
website www.scolarfineart.com
e-mail gsamuel@cwcom.net
Permanent collections include the work of modern and contemporary artists, including Michael Ayrton, David Hockney, Victor Pasmore and Graham Sutherland, and prints by Picasso, Stanley William Hayter, Andy Warhol and many others. Opening hours are 10:00–6:00 Monday–Friday. Scolar Fine Art is wheelchair accessible. Please phone or consult the website for full details of current exhibitions.

London (Sir John Soane's > Tate Britain)

Sir John Soane's Museum, 13 Lincoln's Inn Fields,
London, WC2A 3BP
tel (020) 7405 2107 *fax* (020) 7831 3957
As well as holding the antiquities and works of art collected by Sir John Soane (1753–1837) the museum also plays host to various exhibitions and events throughout the year. 10:00–5:00 Tuesday–Saturday (closed on Sundays, Mondays and bank holidays). In addition, the museum is open 6:00–9:00 on the first Tuesday of every month. Please phone for full details.

Serpentine Gallery, Kensington Gardens, London, W2 3XA
tel (020) 7402 6075 *fax* (020) 7402 4103
website www.serpentinegallery.org
e-mail rosed@serpentinegallery.org
Please phone or consult the website for full details of current exhibitions.

Tate Britain, Millbank, London, SW1P 4RG
tel (020) 7887 8008 *fax* (020) 7887 8007
website www.tate.org.uk
Tate Britain holds the national collection of British art from 1500 to the present day, including the Turner Bequest. Open daily 10:00–5:50 (closed 24–26 December). Admission to the collection displays is free, but there are charges for entry to the exhibitions. Please phone or consult the website for full details of current exhibitions.

- American Sublime*   21 Feb – 19 May 02
- Hamish Fulton*   14 Mar – 2 June 02
- Lucian Freud*   20 June – 15 Sept 02
- Gainsborough*   17 Oct 02 – 12 Jan 03
- Turner Prize 2002*   30 Oct 02 – 5 Jan 03

London (Tate Modern > V&A)

Tate Modern, Bankside, London, SE1 9TG
tel (020) 7887 8008
website www.tate.org.uk
Tate Modern displays the Tate collection of international modern art from 1900 to the present day, including works by Dali, Picasso, Matisse, Rothko and Warhol. Please phone or consult the website for full details of current exhibitions. Open 10:00–6:00 Sunday–Thursday, 10:00–10:00 Friday–Saturday (closed 24–26 December). Admission to the collection is free, but there is a charge for entry to exhibitions.

- The Unilever Commission: Juan Muñoz — To 10 Mar 02
- Andy Warhol — 07 Feb – 01 Apr 02
- Eija Liisa Ahtila — 30 Apr – 28 Jul 02
- Matisse/Picasso — 11 May – 18 Aug 02
- Donald Judd — 19 Sep 02 – 29 Dec 03
- Barnett Newman — 19 Sep 02 – 05 Jan 03
- Performing Objects — 04, 11, 18, 25 Nov

Victoria & Albert Museum, South Kensington, London, SW7 2RL
tel (020) 7942 2000
website www.vam.ac.uk
The V&A is the national museum of art and design, crammed with exhibits from all over the world, including sculpture, ceramics, glass, furniture, metalwork, textiles, paintings, photography, prints, drawings, jewellery and musical instruments. Please phone or consult the website for full details of current exhibitions.

- Radical Fashion* — To 6 Jan 02
- Curvaceous — To 7 Jan 02
- Out of Japan — To 3 Feb 02
- Seeing Things: Photographing Objects 1840–2001 — 20 Feb – Aug 02

London (V&A > Wallace Collection)

- Earth and Fire: Italian Terracotta Sculpture from Donatello to Canova* 14 Mar – July 02
- The Tiara Today* 21 Mar – July 02
- Catherine Walker From May 02

Waddington Galleries Ltd, 11 Cork Street, London, W1S 3LT
tel (020) 7851 2200 *fax* (020) 7734 4146
website www.waddington-galleries.com
e-mail mail@waddington-galleries.com
Waddington Galleries hold a collection of 20th-century paintings, drawings, watercolours and sculpture by British, European and American artists, including Albers, Dubuffet, Matisse, Miró, Moore, Morandi and Picasso, and such contemporary artists as Peter Blake, Patrick Caulfield, Barry Flanagan and Antoni Tàpies. Please phone or consult the website for full details of current exhibitions.

The Wallace Collection, Hertford House, Manchester Square, London, W1M 6BN
tel (020) 7935 0687 *fax* (020) 7224 2155
e-mail admin@the-wallace-collection.org.uk
The Wallace Collection comprises French 18th-century paintings, furniture and porcelain, Old Master paintings, arms and armour, miniatures, French and Italian sculpture, and medieval and Renaissance works of art. Open 10:00–5:00 Monday–Saturday, 12:00–5:00 Sunday. There is full disabled access.
- French Drawings from the Ashmolean Museum, Oxford 16 Jan – 7 Apr 02
- Armour as Art: Treasures of the Wallace Collection 6 June – 22 Sept 02
- Louis XV and his Court 10 Oct 02 – 5 Jan 03

London (Wellington Arch > Zelda Cheatle)

Wellington Arch, Hyde Park Corner, London, W1
tel (020) 7930 2726
Open from 10:00 Wednesday–Sunday and Bank Holidays.
- ■ Photos for the Future 2: Zoom in on London — To 1 Mar 02

Whitechapel Art Gallery, 80–82 Whitechapel High Street, London, E1 7QX
tel (020) 7522 7878 *fax* (020) 7377 1685
website www.whitechapel.org
e-mail info@whitechapel.org
Please phone or consult the website for full details of current exhibitions.
- ■ Mark Wallinger — To 13 Jan 02
- ➤ Nan Goldin* — 25 Jan – 31 Mar 02
  Originated by Centre Georges Pompidou, Paris, and Museo Nacional Centro de Arte Reina Sofia, Madrid

Zelda Cheatle Gallery, 99 Mount Street, London, W1K 2TF
tel (020) 7408 4448 *fax* (020) 7408 1444
e-mail photo@zcgall.demon.co.uk
The gallery specialises in vintage and contemporary British and international fine art photography. Please phone for full details of current exhibitions.
- ■ Manuel Alvarez-Bravo — 15 Jan – 22 Mar 02
- ■ John Deakin — 26 Mar – 24 May 02
- ■ Michael Kenna — 28 May – 26 July 02
- ■ John Davies — 30 July – 20 Sept 02
- ■ Eve Arnold — 24 Sept – 22 Nov 02
- ■ Mark Power — From 26 Nov 02

Machynlleth > Manchester

Machynlleth
The Museum of Modern Art, Wales, Heolt Penrallt, Machynlleth, Powys, SY20 8AJ
tel (01654) 703355 *fax* (01654) 702160
website www.tabernac.dircon.co.uk
e-mail momawales@tabernac.dircon.co.uk

The museum's permanent collection comprises the work of artists living or working in Wales since 1900, including Iwan Bala, Augustus John, Shani Rhys James, Mary Lloyd Jones and Kyffin Williams. Open 10:00–4:00 Monday–Saturday all year except 24–25 December and 1 January. Admission is free, and there is full wheelchair access.

- Winners of 2001 Tabernacle Art Competition — 14 Jan – 9 Feb 02
- Group 75: Spirit of Place* — 18 Feb – 17 Mar 02
- Eleri Mills — 18 Mar – 20 Apr 02
- The Society of Wood Engravers — 25 Mar – 11 May 02
- Gregynog Press — 20 May – 16 June 02
- 2002 Art Competition — 31 July – 7 Sept 02
- Watercolour Society of Wales — 9 Sept – 12 Oct 02
- Catrin Williams and Five Women Artists — 21 Oct 02 – 4 Jan 03

Manchester
Cornerhouse, 70 Oxford Street, Manchester, M1 5NH
tel (0161) 228 7621 *fax* (0161) 200 1506
website www.cornerhouse.org *e-mail* info@cornerhouse.org

Cornerhouse is Greater Manchester's centre for contemporary visual arts, exhibiting work of international significance as well as supporting and promoting artists from the North-West. Opening times are 11:00–6:00 Tuesday–Saturday and 2:00–6:00 Sunday (closed Monday). Please phone for full details of current exhibitions.

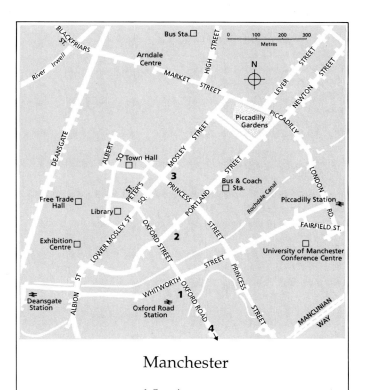

Manchester

1 Cornerhouse
2 The Gallery
3 Manchester City Art Galleries
4 The Whitworth Art Gallery (off map)

Manchester

The Gallery, Manchester's Art House, 131 Portland Street, Manchester, M1 4PY
tel (0161) 237 3551 *fax* (0161) 228 3621
website www.manchestersarthouse.com
e-mail elaine@manchestersarthouse.com
The Gallery specialises in British contemporary fine art, painting, sculpture, furniture, textiles, glass, ceramics and jewellery. Please phone or consult the website for full details of current exhibitions. Opening times are 10:00–5:00 Monday–Friday, 10:00–4:00 Saturday.

Manchester City Art Gallery, Mosley Street, Manchester, M2 3JL
tel (0161) 234 1456 *fax* (0161) 236 7369
website www.cityartgalleries.org.uk
e-mail k.gowland@notes.manchester.gov.uk
Manchester City Art Gallery is closed until early 2002 so that work can take place on a £25 million expansion scheme. Events and activities continue at other venues. Please phone or consult the website for full details.

The Whitworth Art Gallery, University of Manchester, Oxford Road, Manchester, M15 6ER
tel (0161) 275 7450 *fax* (0161) 275 7451
website www.whitworth.man.ac.uk *e-mail* whitworth@man.ac.uk
A diverse and lively programme of changing exhibitions includes selections from the Whitworth's internationally renowned collection of British watercolours, prints, drawings, modern art, sculpture and the largest textile and wallpaper collection outside London. Please phone or consult the website for full details. Opening times are 10:00–5:00 Monday–Saturday, 2:00–5:00 Sunday. Admission is free.

■ Reflecting Japan   To Mar 02

Manchester (Whitworth) > Mansfield

- Views of Germany from the Royal Collection at Windsor Castle — To 10 Mar 02
- Patricia Mackinnon-Day — 17 Jan – 12 Apr 02
- Outsider Art: Work by Untrained Artists — 22 Mar – 2 June 02
- Commonwealth Games Exhibition — June – Sept 02
- Mike Lyons — Sept – Dec 02
- Bawden — Oct – Dec 02

Mansfield

Mansfield Museum & Art Gallery, Leeming Street, Mansfield, Nottinghamshire, NG18 1NG
tel (01623) 463088 *fax* (01623) 412922
website www.mansfield-dc.gov.uk
e-mail mansfield-museum@hotmail.com

The gallery houses the Buxton watercolours, a series of paintings by local artist Albert Sorby Buxton (1867–1932) depicting Mansfield at the beginning of the twentieth century. Please phone for full details of current exhibitions.

- Philip Cox: Paper Sculptures — 5 Jan – 2 Mar 02
- Continuum: Textiles Exhibition — 9 Mar – 13 Apr 02
- ➤ Magic of Masks and Puppets — 20 Apr – 18 June 02
    ➤ *DLI Museum & Durham Art Gallery* ➤ *Mansfield Museum & Art Gallery* ➤ *Rhyl Library, Museum & Art Gallery*
    Originated by Scottish Masks & Puppet Centre
- West Notts College Art Courses Final Year Shows — June 02
- Mansfield Society of Artists — 6 July – 3 Aug 02
- Images 26 Illustration — 10 Aug – 7 Sept 02
- Dodeka: Textiles Exhibition — 14 Sept – 26 Oct 02
- Open Art Exhibition — 2 – 30 Nov 02
- John Allen Textiles — Dec 02

Merthyr Tydfil

Cyfarthfa Castle Museum & Art Gallery, Brecon Road,
Merthyr Tydfil, Mid Glamorgan, CF47 8RE
tel (01685) 723112
The gallery's permanent collection includes works by Sir Cedric Morris, Colin Allen, Kyffin Williams, Brenda Chamberlain, Jack Yeats and Alfred James, as well as by such local artists as Sydney Curnow-Vosper, Penry Williams and George Frederick Harris. Please phone for full details of current exhibitions.

Middlesbrough

Middlesbrough Art Gallery, 320 Linthorpe Road, Middlesbrough, Cleveland, TS1 4AW
tel (01642) 247445 *fax* (01642) 813781
A representative body of work by 20th-century British artists, plus collections of national and international drawings and prizewinners from the Cleveland International Drawing Biennale. Please phone for full details of current exhibitions.

- ■ Ed Pien: Contemporary Drawing Artist*   29 Jan – 13 Mar 02
- ➤ Out of Line: Drawings from the Arts   23 Mar – 11 May 02
  Council Collection*
  NTE from the Hayward Gallery, London
- ➤ Fluid*   18 May – 30 June 02
  ➢ *Wolverhampton Art Gallery* ➢ *Bonnington Gallery, Nottingham*
  ➢ *Middlesbrough Art Gallery*
- ■ Patricia McKinnon Day*   7 Sept – 18 Oct 02
  Originated by Oriel 31, Newtown

Milton Keynes

Milton Keynes Gallery, 900 Midsummer Boulevard, Milton Keynes, Buckinghamshire, MK9 3QA

tel (01908) 676900 *fax* (01908) 558308
website www.mkweb.co.uk/mkg
e-mail mkgallery@mktgc.co.uk
Milton Keynes Gallery provides a purpose-built venue for a changing programme of eight to ten contemporary art exhibitions each year. Please phone or consult the website for full details. Opening hours are 10:00–5:00 Tuesday–Saturday, 12:00–5:00 Sunday. Admission is free.

Much Hadham

The Henry Moore Foundation, Dane Tree House, Perry Green, Much Hadham, Hertfordshire, SG10 6EE
tel (01279) 843 333 *fax* (01279) 843 647
website www.henry-moore-fdn.co.uk
e-mail info@henry-moore-fdn.co.uk
Henry Moore Collections and Exhibitions maintains the Foundation's holding of Moore's work at Perry Green which consists of a major selection of sculpture, drawings and graphics. Open daily by appointment from April to September, visitors may see the artist's studios, outdoor sculptures sited in seventy acres of grounds and the exhibition *Henry Moore: War and Utility in the Sheep Field Barn*.

Nether Stowey

The Court Gallery, Nether Stowey, Somerset, TA5 1NG
tel/fax (01278) 732539
website sourceid.co.uk/court-gallery
The Court Gallery specialises in British Impressionist paintings 1880–1940, the Newlyn, St Ives, Camden Town, Bloomsbury and London groups. Open Monday to Saturday during exhibitions, or by appointment. Please phone or consult the website for full details of current exhibitions.

Newcastle-under-Lyme

Borough Museum & Art Gallery, Brampton Park,
Newcastle-under-Lyme, Staffordshire, ST5 0QP
tel (01782) 619705 *fax* (01782) 855940
website www.newcastle-staffs.gov.uk
e-mail nulmuseum@newcastle-staffs.gov.uk
Opening hours are 10:00–5:30 Monday–Saturday, 2:00–5:30 Sunday.
Closed Good Friday, Bank Holiday Mondays (except Spring Bank
Holiday) and 25 December–1 January inclusive. Admission is free.

- Lorna Bailey — To 27 Jan 02
- Figuratively Speaking: Sculptor Angela Munslow — 5 Jan – 17 Feb 02
- Diane Griffiths — 2 Feb – 3 Mar 02
- Rush on Them: Parodies in Paper — 23 Feb – 3 Mar 02
  Originated by Surrey Institute of Art & Design, Guildford
- Two Arty: Keith and Sue Daulton — 9 Mar – 7 Apr 02

Newcastle upon Tyne

Hatton Gallery, The Quadrangle, University of Newcastle upon Tyne,
Newcastle upon Tyne, Tyne & Wear, NE1 7RU
tel/fax (0191) 222 6059
website www.ncl.ac.uk/hatton *e-mail* hatton-gallery@ncl.ac.uk
The Gallery houses paintings, prints, drawings and sculpture ranging
from the Renaissance to modern times, plus African sculptures and
the Elterwater *Merzbarn* installation by Kurt Schwitters. Please
phone or consult the website for full details of current exhibitions.
Open 10:00–5:30 Monday–Friday, 10:00–4:30 Saturday. Closed Bank
Holidays, Easter Saturday and 27–31 December. Admission is free.

- ➤ Followers of Fashion: Graphic Satires from the Georgian Period* — 12 Jan – 24 Feb 02
  NTE from the Hayward Gallery, London

Laing Art Gallery, New Bridge Street, Newcastle upon Tyne, Tyne & Wear, NE1 8AG
tel (0191) 232 7734 *fax* (0191) 222 0952
e-mail laing@tyne-wear-museums.org.uk
Permanent collection consists of British fine and decorative arts from the 18th century to the present day, including pictures by Reynolds, Landseer, Burne-Jones, Holman Hunt, Bomberg and Spencer. Contemporary works include Kitaj, Auerbach, Ayres and Yass. Please phone for full details of current exhibitions. Open 10:00–5:00 Monday–Saturday, 2:00–5:00 Sunday. Admission free.

- ➤ Beck's Futures 2* To 13 Jan 02
  Originated by ICA Gallery, London
- ■ Centenary Exhibition To 13 Jan 02
- ■ Beauty 9 Feb – 7 Apr 02
- ➤ Light 20 Apr – 7 July 02
  ➤ *Bristol Museum & Art Gallery* ➤ *Laing Art Gallery, Newcastle upon Tyne*

University Gallery, University of Northumbria, Sandyford Road, Newcastle upon Tyne, NE1 8ST
tel (0191) 227 4424 *fax* (0191) 227 4718
e-mail mara-helen.wood@unn.ac.uk
Please phone for full details of current exhibitions.

Newport

Newport Museum & Art Gallery, John Frost Square, Newport, South Wales, NP9 1PA
tel (01633) 840064 *fax* (01633) 222615
e-mail sandra.jackman@newport.gov.uk
The gallery houses permanent collections of 18th- and 19th-century watercolours, topographical engravings, studio ceramics, con-

temporary prints and 19th- and 20th-century paintings. Please phone for full details of current exhibitions.

- ■ Looking Out: Paintings and Drawings by the Welsh Group — To 19 Jan 02
- ■ Brendan Burns — 26 Jan – 9 Mar 02
- ■ Emrys Williams — 23 Mar – 4 May 02
- ■ James Donovan — 18 May – 29 June 02

Newport, IoW

Quay Arts Centre, Sea Street, Newport, Isle of Wight, PO30 5BD
tel (01983) 822490 *fax* (01983) 526606
website www.quayarts.org *e-mail* info@quayarts.demon.co.uk
Please phone or consult the website for full details of current exhibitions.

- ■ Symbiosis — 19 Jan – 23 Feb 02
- ■ Peter Wright: Paintings Retrospective — 6 Apr – 11 May 02
- ■ Hilary Thorpe: Textiles & Paintings — 6 July – 10 Aug 02
- ■ Tim Johnson: Installation & Workshops — 17 Aug – 28 Sept 02

Northampton

Central Museum & Art Gallery, Guildhall Road, Northampton, NN1 1DP
tel (01604) 238548 *fax* (01604) 238720
website www.northampton.gov.uk/museums
e-mail museums@northampton.gov.uk
The gallery possesses an important collection of 15th–18th-century Italian art, including works by Guardi and Giordano. There are also British and Oriental ceramics, early British watercolours, and Norwich School and Pre-Raphaelite works. Modern and contemporary artists are represented by Sickert, Nash, Sutherland, Moore and Hockney. Please phone for full details of current exhibitions.

Norwich

Norwich Gallery, Norwich School of Art & Design, St George Street, Norwich, Norfolk, NR3 1BB
tel (01603) 610561 *fax* (01603) 615728
website www.norwichgallery.co.uk
e-mail nor.gal@nsad.ac.uk
Please phone or consult website for full details of current exhibitions.

Sainsbury Centre for Visual Arts, University of East Anglia, Norwich, Norfolk, NR4 7TJ
tel (01603) 456060 *fax* (01603) 259401
website www.uea.ac.uk/scva *e-mail* scva@uea.ac.uk
The Sainsbury collection combines modern Western art with fine and applied arts from Africa, the Pacific, the Americas, Asia, Egypt, medieval Europe and the ancient Mediterranean. It is particularly well known for its holdings of Francis Bacon, John Davies, Alberto Giacometti and Henry Moore. Please phone or consult the website for full details of current exhibitions.

Nottingham

Angel Row Gallery, Central Library Building, 3 Angel Row, Nottingham, NG1 6HP
tel (0115) 915 2869 *fax* (0115) 915 2860

- Gillian Wearing — To 5 Jan 02
  Originated by the Serpentine Gallery, London
- Carey Young — 12 Jan – 2 Mar 02
- Mali Morris* — 7 May – 29 June 02
- Ravi Depres — 6 July – 2 Nov 02
- Asylum: Places of Refuge — 7 Sept – 2 Nov 02
- Gold Matters* — 9 Nov 02 – 11 Jan 03

Nottingham

Nottingham Castle Museum & Art Gallery,
Nottingham, NG1 6EL
tel (0115) 915 3700 *fax* (0115) 915 3653
website www.nottinghamcity.gov.uk
e-mail samanthah@notmusbhy.demon.co.uk
Over 10,000 works of art including medieval alabasters, Venetian glass, 18th-century silver, English watercolours, studio ceramics and contemporary photography. Please phone or consult the website for full details of current exhibitions.

- Drawing Distinctions* To 27 Jan 02
- Nottingham Studio Group 2 Feb – 17 Mar 02
- National Portrait Gallery Exhibition 27 July – 22 Sept 02
- Nottingham Open Art Exhibition 28 Sept – 13 Oct 02
- Richard Parkes Barington* 25 Oct 02 – 2 Feb 03

Djanogly Art Gallery, Lakeside Arts Centre, University Park, University of Nottingham, Nottingham, NG7 2RD
tel (0115) 951 3192 *fax* (0115) 951 3194
website www.nottingham.ac.uk/artscentre
e-mail neil.bennison@nottingham.ac.uk
Please phone or consult the website for full details of current exhibitions.

- The Golden Age of Watercolours: The Hickman Bacon Collection* 13 Jan – 9 Mar 02
  Originated by the Dulwich Picture Gallery, London
- University Summer Exhibition 29 June – 29 July 02
- ➤ Rubens and Italian Art* 21 Sept – 8 Dec 02
    ➤ *National Gallery of Scotland, Edinburgh* ➤ *Djanogly Art Gallery, Nottingham*

Oldham

Oldham Gallery, Greaves Street, Oldham,
Greater Manchester, OL1 1QN
tel (0161) 911 4657 *fax* (0161) 911 4669
website www.oldham.gov.uk/leisure
e-mail els.art.gallery@oldham.gov.uk
A new state-of-the-art gallery building opens in February 2002.

- Sussed: Sustainability through Creativity   Feb 02 – Feb 03
- Consequences: Contemporary Artists*   Feb – Apr 02
- ➤ Chandrika: Indian Silver Jewellery*   4 May – 6 July 02
   ➤ *Oldham Gallery* ➤ *Harris Museum, Preston* ➤ *Cartwright Hall, Bradford*
- Contemporary Art from Bangladesh*   June – Sept 02
- Timelords: Exploring Concepts and Measures of Time   July – Sept 02
- Clean Rooms: Art and the Biotech Industry*   Sept – Nov 02
- A Passing Flower: Wild Flowers in Art*   Dec 02 – Mar 03

Oxford

Ashmolean Museum, Beaumont Street, Oxford, OX1 2PH
tel (01865) 278000 *fax* (01865) 278018
website www.ashmol.ox.ac.uk
The United Kingdom's oldest public museum displays the University's rich collections of antiquities, paintings, drawings, sculpture, silver, ceramics, textiles, musical instruments, coins and metalwork, ranging over four millennia. Admission is free.

- Opulence and Devotion: Brazilian Baroque Art*   To 3 Feb 02

Oxford (Ashmolean)

- Acts of Faith: Brazilian Contemporary Photography* To 3 Feb 02
- Bolognese Drawings from Stockholm* 5 Mar – 26 May 02
- Illustrators of the *Radio Times** 11 June – 7 Sept 02
- ➤ Travelling Companions: Hals and Manet* 28 Sept – 24 Nov 02
  Originated by the National Gallery, London

Christ Church Picture Gallery, Christ Church,
Oxford, OX1 1DP
tel (01865) 276172 *fax* (01865) 202429
website www.chch.ox.ac.uk
e-mail dennis.harrington@christ-church.ox.ac.uk
Christ Church Picture Gallery houses an internationally important collection of Old Master paintings and drawings, especially famous for its Italian pieces, which range from the early Renaissance to the 18th century and include works by Leonardo da Vinci, Michelangelo, Raphael, Veronese, Tintoretto and the Carracci. Please phone for full details of current exhibitions.

Museum of Modern Art, 30 Pembroke Street,
Oxford, OX1 1BP
tel (01865) 722733 *fax* (01865) 722573
website www.moma.org.uk
e-mail info@moma.org.uk
Please phone or consult website for full details of current exhibitions.

- Ed Ruscha* To 13 Jan 02
- ➤ Trauma* 26 Jan – 7 Apr 02
  NTE from Hayward Gallery, London

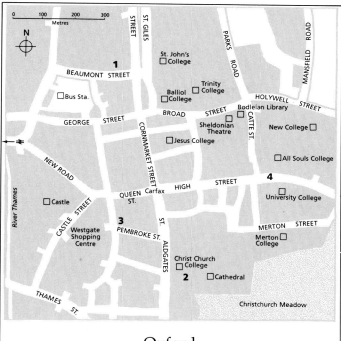

Oxford

1 Ashmolean Museum, University of Oxford

2 Christ Church Picture Gallery

3 Museum of Modern Art

4 Oxford Gallery

Oxford > Perth

Pitt Rivers Museum, Parks Road, Oxford, OX1 3PP
tel (01865) 270927 *fax* (01865) 270943
website www.prm.ox.ac.uk *e-mail* prm@prm.ox.ac.uk
The Pitt Rivers Museum is famous for its unique period atmosphere and its collections of archaeological and anthropological artefacts from all parts of the world and all periods of history. Please phone or consult the website for full details of current exhibitions. Open 1:00–4:30 Monday–Saturday, 2:00–4:30 Sunday.

- Transformations: The Art of Recycling* To 1 June 02
- Open Voices Project: Objects and Identities Oct 02 – Oct 03

Penarth

Turner House Gallery, Plymouth Road, Penarth,
South Glamorgan, CF64 3DM
tel (029) 2070 8870
website www.nmgw.ac.uk
Please phone or consult the website for full details of current exhibitions.

- South Wales Arts Society To 27 Jan 02
- Watercolour Society of Wales 2 Feb – 31 Mar 02

Perth

The Fergusson Gallery, Marshall Place, Perth, PH2 8NU
tel (01738) 441944 *fax* (01738) 621152
e-mail museum@pkc.gov.uk
Devoted to the work of Scottish colourist painter J. D. Fergusson (1874–1961), the Fergusson Gallery offers a changing programme of thematic exhibitions of his paintings, drawings, photographs and sculptures. Research and archive facilities are available by appointment. Please phone for full details of current exhibitions.

- Drawing from Experience To Mar 02

Perth (Fergusson) > Peterborough

- J. D. Fergusson Arts Awards Trust Winner 2001* To Apr 02
- Celtic Spirit To Apr 02

Perth Museum & Art Gallery, 78 George Street, Perth, PH1 5LB
tel (01738) 632488 *fax* (01738) 443505
website www.pkc.gov.uk *e-mail* museum@pkc.gov.uk
Perth Museum & Art Gallery presents an extensive collection of mainly Scottish paintings, prints, drawings, watercolours and sculpture from the 16th century to the present day. Artists represented include Thomas Laurence, Laura Knight, Horatio McCulloch, William McTaggart, D. Y. Cameron, J. E. Millais, Beatrix Potter, John Eardley and Anne Redpath. Open 10:00–5:00 Monday–Saturday (closed Christmas and New Year). Admission is free.

- Change: The Development of Scottish Art To 27 Apr 02
- New Faces: Works added to the Permanent Collection during 2001 To 27 Apr 02
- Fact or Fancy: History Paintings To 27 Apr 02
- Perth Festival of the Arts 2002 17 May – 15 June 02
- D. O. Hill Bi-Centenary 1802–2002* 6 July – Oct 02
- Perthshire Art Association Annual Exhibition* 25 Oct – 23 Nov 02
- Scottish Council for Independent Schools Art & Design Show* 14 Dec 02 – 25 Jan 03

Peterborough

Peterborough Museum & Art Gallery, Priestgate, Peterborough, Cambridgeshire, PE1 1LF
tel (01733) 343329 *fax* (01733) 341928
website www.peterboroughheritage.org.uk
e-mail museum@peterborough.gov.uk

Peterborough (Museum) > Plymouth

A varied programme of art and craft exhibitions including video and multi-media. Please phone or consult the website for full details.

Plymouth
New Street Gallery, 38 New Street, The Barbican, Plymouth, Devon, PL1 2NA
tel (01752) 221450
The New Street Gallery hosts exhibitions of leading contemporary artists from the West Country including Bryan Pearce, Robert Lenkiewicz, Mary Stork, Derek Holland, Diane Nevitt, Louise McClary, Tony O'Malley and Fred Yates. Please phone for full details of current exhibitions.
- Mary Martin   Easter 02
- Sarah Gillespie   Autumn 02

Plymouth City Museum & Art Gallery, Drake Circus, Plymouth, Devon, PL4 8AJ
tel (01752) 304774 *fax* (01752) 304775
e-mail museum@plymouth.gov.uk
As well as housing the Cottonian Collection of oil paintings (including works by Reynolds, Kauffmann, Ruysdael, Laroon and Van Der Velde), permanent collections include paintings from the Newlyn School and the St Ives and Camden Town groups, Old Master drawings and prints, figurines, manuscripts, furniture, Chinese ceramics, Plymouth porcelain and Staffordshire pottery.
- Polish Ground: Photography by Paul Warner FRPS   To end Feb 02
- Maritime Paintings from the Collection   To end Dec 02
- Camden Town Paintings from the Collection   mid Jan – mid Apr 02
- ➤ Words*   4 May – 20 July 02
    Originated by the Arts Council, London

Plymouth (City Museum) > Preston

■ Brian Rice Retrospective* Nov 02 – Spring 03

Pontefract

Pontefract Museum, 5 Salter Row, Pontefract,
West Yorkshire, WF8 1BA
tel (01977) 722740 *fax* (01977) 722742
Please phone for full details of current exhibitions.

Portsmouth

Aspex Gallery, Aspex Visual Arts Trust, 27 Brougham Road,
Southsea, Portsmouth, Hampshire, PO5 4PA
tel (02392) 812121 *fax* (02392) 812121
website aspex.org.uk *e-mail* info@aspex.org.uk
A contemporary art gallery, the Aspex mounts approximately six shows a year. Please phone or consult website for full details of current exhibitions.

Preston

Harris Museum & Art Gallery, Market Square, Preston,
Lancashire, PR1 2PP
tel (01772) 258248 *fax* (01772) 886764
website www.preston.gov.uk/harris
e-mail harris.museum@preston.gov.uk
Collections include British paintings and watercolours of the 17th–20th centuries, drawings (including 16th- and 17th-century Old Masters), prints (including many Old Masters and political cartoons), artists' sketchbooks, miniatures, silhouettes, illuminated manuscripts and sculpture. Please phone or consult the website for full details of current exhibitions.

■ European Drawings from the Collection To Jan 02
■ Horrickses Fashions Ltd To Oct 02

- Junichi Arki: Rotunda Commission — Feb 02
- UCLan Fine Art MA Show* — 13 Apr – 11 May 02
- Art South Asia: Pakistan — June – Sept 02

Rhyl

Rhyl Library, Museum & Art Gallery, Church Street, Rhyl, Denbighshire, LL18 3AA
tel (01745) 353814 *fax* (01745) 331438
e-mail andrea.rhylartscentre@denbighshire.dot.gov.uk

- Why Did I Buy That? — To 5 Jan 02
- Gerald Gadd — To 5 Jan 02
- Ian Williams — 12 Jan – 23 Feb 02
- Denbigh Historical Society — 12 Jan – 23 Feb 02
- Nicole Faleur — 2 Mar – 13 Apr 02
- ➤ Spotlight on Kenneth Martin — 2 Mar – 1 June 02
  NTE from Hayward Gallery, London
- Tim Pugh — 20 Apr – 18 May 02
- Llandrillo College — 22 June – 8 July 02
- Hafen Deg — 20 July – 3 Aug 02
- ➤ Magic of Masks and Puppets — 31 Aug – 12 Oct 02
  ➤ DLI Museum & Durham Art Gallery ➤ Mansfield Museum & Art Gallery ➤ Rhyl Library, Museum & Art Gallery
  Originated by the Scottish Masks & Puppet Centre

Rochdale

Rochdale Art Gallery, Esplanade Arts & Heritage Centre, Rochdale, Greater Manchester, OL16 1AQ
tel/fax (01706) 342154
e-mail artgallery@rochdale.gov.uk
The gallery is closed for refurbishment until mid-2002. Please phone for full details.

Ross-on-Wye

Cornelius Gallery, Ross-on-Wye Antiques Centre, Gloucester Road, Ross-on-Wye, Herefordshire, HR9 5BU
tel (01989) 762290 *fax* (01989) 762291
Please phone for full details of current exhibitions.

Rotherham

Rotherham Art Gallery, Rotherham Arts Centre, Walker Place, Rotherham, South Yorkshire, S65 1JH
tel (01709) 823624 *fax* (01709) 823653
website www.rma.org *e-mail* david.gilbert@rotherham.gov.uk
The gallery's fine art collection is based around a bequest of oils and watercolours gifted in 1908, and features artists such as Dame Ethel Walker, George Romney, William Cowen, Edwin La Dell and H. H. La Thangue. Please phone or consult the website for full details of current exhibitions.

- ■ Kate Scully and Jenny Savage   7 Jan – 9 Feb 02
- ■ Charles Monkhouse   14 Feb – 23 Mar 02
- ■ Arthouse Members   28 Mar – 27 Apr 02

Rugby

Rugby Art Gallery, Museum & Library, Little Elborow Street, Rugby, Warwickshire, CV21 3BZ
tel (01788) 533201 *fax* (01788) 533204
website www.rugbygalleryandmuseum.org.uk
e-mail rugbyartgallery&museum@rugby.gov.uk
The 400 square metre gallery hosts a programme of changing exhibitions, including national and local art and crafts and Rugby's own Collection of Modern Art, which includes work by such artists as Stanley Spencer and L. S. Lowry. Please phone or consult the website for full details of current exhibitions.

St Andrews

Crawford Arts Centre, 93 North Street, St Andrews,
Fife, KY16 9AD
tel (01334) 474610 *fax* (01334) 479880
website www.crawfordarts.free-online.co.uk
e-mail crawfordarts@crawfordarts.free-online.co.uk

- David Tremlett* — 18 Jan – 10 Mar 02
- Museum/Gallery Studies Students' Exhibition* — 15 Mar – 5 May 02
- ➤ Philomaena Pretsele* — 10 May – 30 June 02
  ➤ *Crawford Arts Centre, St Andrews* ➤ *Paisley Museum*
- Scottish Touring Exhibition Consortium Show* — 5 July – 25 Aug 02
- Summer Craft — 5 July – 25 Aug 02
- Football Haiku* — 30 Aug – 20 Oct 02
- Christmas Craft — 1 Nov – 20 Dec 02

St Ives

Barbara Hepworth Museum & Sculpture Garden, Barnoon Hill,
St Ives, Cornwall, TR26 1TG
tel (01736) 796226 *fax* (01736) 794480
website www.tate.org.uk

When Barbara Hepworth died in 1975 her will asked that Trewyn Studios and the adjacent garden, complete with a selection of her sculptures, be permanently opened to the public. The museum and garden offer a remarkable insight into the work and outlook of one of Britain's most important 20th-century artists.

Tate St Ives, Porthmeor Beach, St Ives, Cornwall, TR26 1TG
tel (01736) 796226 *fax* (01736) 794480
website www.tate.org.uk

St Ives (Tate) > **Salford**

The Tate St Ives presents a programme of 20th-century paintings and sculpture associated with St Ives, drawn from the Tate Gallery collection. Artists represented include Wallis, Nicholson, Hepworth, Gabo, Frost, Heron, Wells and Barns-Graham. Open 10:30–5:30 Tuesday–Sunday, plus Mondays in July–August and most Bank Holidays (closed 30 October–12 November and 24–26 December).

- Sandra Blow* — To 3 Mar 02
- Vicken Parsons* — To 3 Mar 02
- Ian Hamilton Finlay* — 11 Mar – 2 June 02
- Simon Starling* — 11 Mar – 2 June 02
- Hussein Chalayan* — 11 Mar – 2 June 02
- Richard Long* — 10 June – 1 Sept 02
- Naum Gabo* — 10 June – 1 Sept 02

Salford

Ordsall Hall Museum, 322 Ordsall Lane, Salford, Greater Manchester, M5 3EX
tel (0161) 872 0251 *fax* (0161) 872 4951
website www.ordsallhall.org
e-mail admin@ordsallhall.org

This 600-year-old building is one of the finest examples of Tudor architecture in the region. There are temporary exhibitions and events throughout the year. Please phone or consult the website for details. Open 10:00–4:00 Monday–Friday, 1:00–4:00 Sunday. Admission is free. Limited disabled access.

Salford Museum & Art Gallery, Peel Park, The Crescent, Salford, Greater Manchester, M5 4WU
tel (0161) 736 2649 *fax* (0161) 745 9490
website www.salfordmuseum.org
e-mail salford.museum@salford.gov.uk

Contemporary and Victorian fine and decorative arts are displayed, while temporary exhibition spaces show a wide variety of art throughout the year. There is adjacent parkland. Open 10:00–4:45 Monday–Friday, 1:00–5:00 Saturday–Sunday. Disabled access. Admission is free. Please phone or consult the website for full details of current exhibitions.

Scunthorpe

Normanby Hall Country Park, Normanby Hall, Normanby, Scunthorpe, North Lincolnshire, DN15 9HU
tel (01724) 720588
website www.northlincs.gov.uk\museums
Normanby Hall is a Regency house open to the public from April to October, furnished in the Regency style. Notable pieces include a Gillows bookcase and paintings by Rubens, Lawrance Mytens and Kneller. A costume gallery holds annually changing exhibitions. Please phone or consult the website for full details.

North Lincolnshire Museum, Oswald Road, Scunthorpe, North Lincolnshire, DN15 7BD
tel (01724) 843533 *fax* (01724) 270474
The museum hosts a lively programme of exhibitions, events and lectures. Please phone for full details.

Selkirk

Bowhill Art Gallery, Bowhill House, Selkirk, Borders, TD7 5ET
tel/fax (01750) 22204
website www.heritageontheweb.co.uk *e-mail* bht@buccleuch.com
Open 1:00–4:30 every day in July and by appointment for educational groups throughout the year. The collection includes paintings by Reynolds, Gainsborough, Canaletto, Guardi, Van Dyck,

Lely and Raeburn, miniatures by Cooper, Oliver and Holbein, and porcelain, silver, tapestries and fine French furniture.

Sheffield

Graves Art Gallery, Surrey Street, Sheffield, South Yorkshire, S1 1XZ
tel (0114) 278 2600 *fax* (0114) 273 4705
website www.sheffieldgalleries.org.uk
e-mail info@sheffieldgalleries.org.uk
A regional centre for touring exhibitions and home to Sheffield's outstanding collection of late 19th- and 20th-century European art and 20th-century British art, by artists including Matisse, Bonnard, Nash and Spencer.

- ➤ Nigel Henderson: Parallel of Life and Art   To 2 Feb 02
  - ➢ *Graves Art Gallery, Sheffield* ➢ *Dean Gallery, Edinburgh*
  - *Originated by Gainsborough's House, Sudbury*
- ➤ Jeremy Moon: A Retrospective Exhibition   To 2 Mar 02
  - *Originated by Handwork Touring*
- ■ Pilgrimage   16 Feb – 13 Apr 02
- ■ Terence Donovan   25 May – 3 Aug 02
- ➤ Leonardo Drawings from the Royal   12 July – 21 Sept 02
  Collection
  - ➢ *Lady Lever Art Gallery, Liverpool* ➢ *Swansea* ➢ *Graves Art Gallery, Sheffield*
- ■ Garry Fabian Miller Photographs   17 Aug – 12 Oct 02
- ■ Exploring Landscape   26 Oct 02 – end Jan 03

Mappin Art Gallery, Weston Bank, Sheffield, South Yorkshire, S10 2TP
tel (0114) 278 2600 *fax* (0114) 275 0957
website www.sheffieldgalleries.org.uk
e-mail info@sheffieldgalleries.org.uk

Sheffield (Mappin)

The Mappin's galleries contain Old Masters and 18th–19th-century paintings from the city's collection, alongside exhibitions of cutting-edge contemporary art. Open 10:00–5:00 Tuesday–Saturday, 11:00–5:00 Sunday.

- ■ Sacred and Profane — To 14 Jan 02
- ■ Richard Wilson: Irons in the Fire — 19 Jan – 21 Apr 02
- ■ Mappin Open Solo Show: Andrew Cranston — 19 Jan – 21 Apr 02
- ■ International Mappin Open — 4 May – 28 July 02
- ■ New Contemporaries — Nov – Dec 02

Millennium Galleries, Arundel Gate, Sheffield, South Yorkshire, S1 2PP
tel (0114) 278 2600 *fax* (0114) 278 2604
website www.sheffieldgalleries.org.uk
e-mail info@sheffieldgalleries.org.uk

Millennium Galleries permanent collection aims to bring world class art, craft and design to Sheffield and the surrounding region. The building contains four galleries, housing major touring exhibitions alongside displays from Sheffield's own collections. Please phone or consult the website for full details of current exhibitions.

- ➤ Cutting Edge: A History of British Cutlery and Place Settings* — 11 Jan – 10 Mar 02
  ➢ Fairfax House, York ➢ Millennium Galleries, Sheffield ➢ Geffrye Museum, London
- ➤ Movies on the Move — 9 Feb – 12 May 02
  Organised by Museum of the Moving Image
- ■ The Porcelain Room: An Installation by Edmund de Waal — May 02
- ■ The Power of the Poster — 8 June – 22 Sept 02
- ■ 2D–3D National Exhibition of Theatre Design — Oct – Dec 02

Southampton

John Hansard Gallery, University of Southampton, Highfield, Southampton, Hampshire, SO17 1BJ
tel (02380) 592158 *fax* (02380) 594192
e-mail hansard@soton.ac.uk

- ➤ Gina Pane* — To 19 Jan 02
  - *John Hansard Gallery, Southampton* ➤ *Arnolfini, Bristol*
- ■ Critical Interventions III: Unprincipled Passions — 5 Feb – 23 Mar 02
- ➤ Michael Snow* — 23 Apr – 8 June 02
  - *Arnolfini, Bristol* ➤ *John Hansard Gallery, Southampton*
- ■ Potential* — 25 June – 24 Aug 02
- ■ Again Again* — 10 Sept – 26 Oct 02

Southampton City Art Gallery, Civic Centre, Southampton, Hampshire, SO14 7LP
tel (023 80) 832277 *fax* (023 80) 832153
website www.southampton.gov.uk/leisure/arts
e-mail art.gallery@southampton.gov.uk

Southampton City Art Gallery hosts a major collection of British and European paintings from the 14th–20th centuries. Displays are changed regularly so that the scope of the collection, from Old Masters to contemporary British art, can be viewed during the course of a year. Please phone or consult the website for full details of current exhibitions.

- ■ Paul Morrison — 7 Feb – 14 Apr 02
- ■ William Ratcliffe & Harold Gilman — 25 Apr – 2 June 02
- ■ Douglas Allsop — 13 June – 8 Sept 02
- ■ Thoroughly Modern Women: Women in British Modernism 1900–1945 — Oct – Dec 02

Southport > Stevenage

Southport

Atkinson Art Gallery, Lord Street, Southport,
Merseyside, PR9 7NB
tel (01704) 533133 *fax* (0151) 934 2109
e-mail www.seftonarts.co.uk
The Atkinson's permanent collection includes Victorian watercolours and oils, and work by 20th-century artists, including L. S. Lowry. The gallery also has a small collection of sculpture, including work by Henry Moore. Please phone for full details of current exhibitions.

- Southport Palette Club: Artwork by Local Painters*   4 Feb – 2 Mar 02
- Southport Photographic Society*   16 Mar – 6 Apr 02

Stevenage

Boxfield Gallery, Stevenage Arts & Leisure Centre, Lytton Way, Stevenage, Hertfordshire, SG1 1LZ
tel (01438) 242652 *fax* (01438) 242342
e-mail william.barnard@stevenage-leisure.co.uk
Full disabled access.

- Nelina Sharp: Four Seasons   To 6 Jan 02
- Belarus Artists   11 Jan – 10 Feb 02
- Shara Moray   15 Feb – 17 Mar 02
- Apollo Group   22 Mar – 21 Apr 02
- Boxfield Prize   26 Apr – 26 May 02
- Age Concern Exhibition   28 May – 7 June 02
- Stevenage Arts Festival   28 May – 23 June 02
- International Association of Astronomical Artists   28 June – 27 July 02
- Iberhim Wagh   2 Aug – 1 Sept 02
- Lizanne Van Essen   6 Sept – 6 Oct 02

Stirling

The Smith Art Gallery & Museum, Dumbarton Road, Stirling, Grampian, FK8 2RQ
tel (01786) 471917 *fax* (01786) 449523
website www.smithartgallery.demon.co.uk
e-mail museum@smithartgallery.demon.co.uk

The Smith holds a fine collection of 19th-century British and European art, including English watercolours, Norwich School, Scottish art, Glasgow School, Hague School, French salon paintings, and 20th-century and some contemporary Scottish paintings. Open 10:30–5:00 Tuesday–Saturday, 2:00–5:00 Sunday. Admission is free.

- Scottish Photographic Federation*   11 May – 2 June 02
- Stitched Art: Embroiderers' Guild Exhibition* 16 Nov 02 – 5 Jan 03

Stockport

Stockport Art Gallery, Wellington Road South, Stockport, Greater Manchester, SK3 8AB
tel (0161) 474 4453 *fax* (0161) 480 4960
e-mail stockport.art.gallery@stockport.gov.uk

Opening hours are 11:00–5:00 Monday–Tuesday and Thursday–Friday, 10:00–5:00 Saturday. Open on Bank Holidays except Christmas Day, Boxing Day and New Year's Day. Admission is free.

- Stockport Art Guild Annual Exhibition   To 5 Jan 02
- Hillary Jack: Recent Paintings   12 Jan – 9 Feb 02
- Chain: Real Life Art Practice   12 Jan – 9 Feb 02
- Sefton Guild of Artists   16 Feb – 16 Mar 02
- Stockport Secondary Schools and Sixth Form Colleges Art Exhibition   16 Feb – 16 Mar 02
- Stockport Photographic Society Annual Exhibition   23 Mar – 20 Apr 02

Stockport (Art Gallery) > Stoke-on-Trent

- Barry White Paintings — 23 Mar – 20 Apr 02
- Cath Prior Photographs — 27 Apr – 25 May 02
- Gareth Mason Sculpture — 27 Apr – 25 May 02
- Alan Waters Sculpture — 27 Apr – 25 May 02
- Stockport College Design Shows — 1 – 25 June 02
- Stockport Open Exhibition — 11 July – 31 Aug 02
- *Stockport Express & Times* Photographs — 7 Sept – 5 Oct 02
- Michael Anderson Paintings — 7 Sept – 5 Oct 02
- Stockport Art Guild Exhibition — 24 Nov 02 – 4 Jan 03
- XRX Christmas Craft Show — 23 Nov 02 – 4 Jan 03

Stoke-on-Trent

Alsager Gallery, Department of Contemporary Art, Manchester Metropolitan University, Hassall Road, Alsager, Stoke-on-Trent, Cheshire, ST7 2HL
tel (0161) 247 5302 *fax* (0161) 247 6377
Open 9:00–5:00. Please phone for full details of current exhibitions.

- Ambivalence: Mark Parkinson — To Jan 02
- Off the Shelf: Sarah Nicholson — Feb 02
- Armour/Amour: Susan Cutts — Mar 02

The Potteries Museum & Art Gallery, Bethseda Street, Hanley, Stoke-on-Trent, ST1 3DW
tel (01782) 232323 *fax* (01782) 232500
website www.stoke.gov.uk/museums *e-mail* museums@stoke.gov.uk
The Potteries Museum and Art Gallery contains the world's finest collection of Staffordshire ceramics, with over 5000 pieces on permanent display, plus an important collection of 20th-century British art, ranging from Sickert and Lowry to Grayson Perry and Mark Wallinger. Please phone or consult the website for full details of current exhibitions.

Stoke-on-Trent (The Potteries) > Sudbury

- ► Out of Line: Drawings from the Arts Council Collection
  NTE from Hayward Gallery, London — 2 Feb – 17 Mar 02
- ■ John Currie and British Art from the Tate* — 30 Mar – 9 June 02
- ■ Susie Cooper — 4 May – 30 June 02
- ■ Jerwood Applied Arts Prize: Ceramics — 7 Sept – 3 Nov 02

The Wedgwood Museum, Barlaston, Stoke-on-Trent, ST12 9ES
tel (01782) 282818 *fax* (01782) 223315
website www.wedgwoodmuseum.org.uk
e-mail wedgwood.museum@wedgwood.co.uk
The museum is closed until mid-2003 for major refurbishment.

Stromness

Pier Arts Centre, 28–30 Victoria Street, Stromness, Orkney, KW16 3AA
tel (01856) 850209 *fax* (01856) 851462
e-mail info@pierartscentre.com
Holds a permanent collection of 20th-century British art, including works by Ben Nicholson, Barbara Hepworth, Sir Terry Frost, Patrick Heron, Alan Davie, Margaret Mellis and Alfred Wallis. Please phone for full details of current exhibitions.

Sudbury

Gainsborough's House, 46 Gainsborough Street, Sudbury, Suffolk, CO10 7EU
tel (01787) 372958 *tel* (01787) 376991
website www.gainsborough.org *e-mail* mail@gainsborough.org
This birthplace museum holds a collection of works reflecting all aspects of Thomas Gainsborough's imagination, including portraits

Sudbury (Gainsborough's House) > Swansea

and landscapes, drawings, innovative prints, and even a sculpture. The reserve collection includes work by Gainsborough's teachers and peers, including Hayman, Gravelot and Gainsborough Dupont. Please phone or consult the website for full details of current exhibitions.

- ➤ Mount Fuji: Photographs by Chris Steele-Perkins* 23 Mar – 12 May 02
  - ➤ *MAC, Birmingham* ➤ *Gainsborough's House, Sudbury*
- ■ Gainsborough Pop Autumn 02
- ■ Gainsborough House Printmakers Winter 02

Sunderland

Northern Gallery for Contemporary Art, City Library & Art Centre, 28–30 Fawcett Street, Sunderland, SR1 1RG
tel (0191) 524 1235 *fax* (0191) 514 8444
website www.ngca.co.uk
e-mail joanna.rowlands@edcom.sunderland.gov.uk
The Northern Gallery runs an innovative programme of contemporary art exhibitions, displaying the work of emerging as well as internationally recognised artists. Please phone or consult the website for full details of current exhibitions.

Swansea

Oriel Ceri Richards Gallery, Taliesin Arts Centre, University College, Swansea, SA2 8PZ
tel (01792) 295526 *fax* (01792) 295899
website www.taliesinartscentre.co.uk
e-mail s.e.crouch@swansea.ac.uk

- ■ Janet Bligh: New Work 18 Jan – 16 Feb 02
- ■ Andrea Kelland and Angela Hoppe Kingston 5 Apr – 4 May 02

- Artists of Kosovo   10 May – 8 June 02
- Ogwyn Davies: 'Gwlad'   23 Aug – 21 Sept 02

Swindon

Swindon Museum & Art Gallery, Bath Road, Old Town, Swindon, Wiltshire, SN1 4BA
tel (01793) 466556 *fax* (01793) 484141
website www.swindon.gov.uk

The gallery houses a wide range of paintings, watercolours, drawings, prints, photographs and studio pottery, plus a small amount of sculpture. Artists represented include Terry Frost, Howard Hodgkin, Gwen and Augustus John, Maggi Hambling, W. R. Sickert, Ivon Hitchens, Christopher Le Brun and Lisa Milroy. Please phone or consult the website for full details of current exhibitions.

- It's a Gift   To Mar 02
- Narrative Paintings   Mar 02

Taunton

Brewhouse, Coal Orchard, Taunton, Somerset, TA1 1JL
tel/fax (01823) 323116
website www.brewhouse-theatre.co.uk
e-mail brewhouse@btconnect.com

The centre's Phillips Gallery presents on average seven exhibitions or artists' projects per year, each lasting six to eight weeks. The Brewhouse also has a studio and darkroom, used for educational purposes with the aim of encouraging integration between the performing, creative and visual arts. Please phone for full details of current exhibitions.

- Atmosphere: New Fibre Art and California Fibers   5 Jan – 9 Feb 02
- Sue Bleakley   16 Feb – 30 Mar 02

Taunton (Brewhouse) > Truro

- Group Show featuring Sue Wyllie — 4 Apr – 11 May 02
- James Ravilious and Chris Willoughby — 18 May – 29 June 02

Tenby

Tenby Museum & Art Gallery, Castle Hill, Tenby, Pembrokeshire, Dyfed, SA70 7BP
tel/fax (01834) 842809
e-mail tenbymuseum@hotmail.com

The permanent collection consists predominantly of work by local artists, such as Gwen and Augustus John, Nina Hamnett and Charles Norris. Please phone for full details of current exhibitions.

Truro

Lemon Street Gallery, 13 Lemon Street, Truro, Cornwall, TR1 2LS
tel (01872) 275757 *fax* (01637) 875611
website www.lemonstreetgallery.co.uk
e-mail lemonstreetgallery@btinternet.com

The permanent collection includes work by Sandra Blow, John Hoyland, Kurt Jackson, Barbara Rae, John Bellany, Hamish MacDonald, Emma Davis, Carlo Rossi, David Briggs, Anthony Frost, Louise McClary and Peter Howson, plus silverware, jewellery, ceramics and sculpture.

- Affordable Art Show* — 18 Jan – 11 Feb 02
- Rachael Jeffreys* — 15 Feb – 11 Mar 02
- Easter Exhibition* — 15 Mar – 29 Apr 02
- Ronald Smith and Jason Walker* — 3 May – 3 June 02
- Royal Academy Show* — 7 June – 1 July 02
- Summer Exhibition* — 5 July – 19 Aug 02
- ➤ Kurt Jackson* — 23 Aug – 23 Sept 02
    - ➤ R. G. Kelly Gallery, Glasgow ➤ Dundas Street Gallery, Edinburgh
    - ➤ Lemon Street Gallery, Truro

Truro (Lemon Street) > Uppingham

- Glen Scouller*   27 Sept – 21 Oct 02
- David Briggs   25 Oct – 18 Nov 02
- Christmas Show   22 Nov 02 – 22 Jan 03

Royal Cornwall Museum, River Street, Truro, Cornwall, TR1 2SJ
tel (01872) 272205   *fax* (01872) 240514
website www.royalcornwallmuseum.co.uk
e-mail enquiries@royalcornwallmuseum.freeserve.co.uk
The museum holds a pre-eminent collection of ceramics and hosts a changing display of fine and decorative art, as well as a diverse programme of temporary exhibitions ranging from photographs and textiles to Old Masters and natural history. Please phone or consult website for full details of current exhibitions.

- Amish Quilts   To Jan 02
- Serena Banham   To Jan 02
- Association of British Decorative Silversmiths Silver Show   To Jan 02
- Cornwall Wildlife Trust Photographs   Feb 02
- St Ives Printmakers   Feb – Mar 02
- Ceramica: An International Festival of Clay   May – June 02
- Embroiderers' Guild   July 02
- Helen Parrott   July 02
- David Tovey Paintings   Aug 02
- Kurt Jackson Paintings   Oct – Nov 02

Uppingham

Goldmark Gallery, Orange Street, Uppingham, Rutland, LE15 9SQ
tel (01572) 821424   *fax* (01572) 821503
e-mail mike@mgoldmark.freeserve.co.uk
The permanent collection includes work by Marc Chagall, Eric Gill,

Uppingham (Goldmark) > Wakefield

James Gillray, Patrick Caulfield, Graham Sutherland, Rigby Graham, John Piper and many others. Please phone for full details of current exhibitions.

Wakefield

Wakefield Art Gallery, Wentworth Terrace, Wakefield, West Yorkshire, WF1 3QW
tel (01924) 305900 *fax* (01924) 305770
Permanent collection includes sculptures by Henry Moore and Barbara Hepworth, and early 20th-century paintings. Please phone for full details of current exhibitions.

- ➤ Edward Ardizzone: Etchings and Lithographs* To 6 Jan 02
  ➤ Wakefield Art Gallery ➤ Durham Art Gallery ➤ Royal Museum & Art Gallery, Canterbury
  Originated by Wolseley Fine Arts, London
- ■ This England: Photographs by Richard Batty 19 Jan – 3 Mar 02
- ■ Local Art Clubs 16 Mar – 28 Apr 02
- ■ Muriel Metcalfe 11 May – 23 June 02
- ■ Animals in A4 6 July – 1 Sept 02

Wakefield Museum, Wood Street, Wakefield, West Yorkshire, WF1 2EW
tel (01924) 305356 *fax* (01924) 305353
Refurbished in 2000 to provide an interactive experience. The ground floor gallery features the Charles Waterton Collection. Please phone for full details of current exhibitions.

- ■ A Century of Electricity 14 Jan – 17 Mar 02
- ■ Something Old Something New 30 Mar – 9 June 02
- ■ Small Found Objects of Desire 14 Sept – 17 Nov 02

Wakefield > Walsall

Yorkshire Sculpture Park, Bretton Hall, West Bretton, Wakefield, West Yorkshire, WF4 4LG
tel (01924) 830302 *fax* (01924) 830044
website www.ysp.co.uk *e-mail* office@ysp.co.uk
Changing displays of modern and contemporary sculpture are organised throughout the park. The collection includes work by Borofsky, Card, Davey, Frink, Hepworth, King, Lewitt, Nash, Serra, Shapiro, Tucker and Wentworth. A display of large bronzes by Henry Moore can be seen in neighbouring Bretton Country Park. Please phone or consult the website for full details of current exhibitions.

Walsall

The New Art Gallery, Gallery Square, Walsall, West Midlands, WS2 8LG
tel (01922) 654400 *fax* (01922) 654401
website www.artatwalsall.org.uk
e-mail info@artatwalsall.org.uk
The gallery's collection is based on the Garman Ryan bequest, donated in 1974 by Lady Kathleen Garman, widow of Sir Jacob Epstein, and sculptor Sally Ryan. There are works by Epstein himself, as well as by Van Gogh, Modigliani, Picasso, Gericault, Delacroix, Monet, Degas and other renowned artists.

- 40 Part Motet — To 13 Jan 02
- Gifts to Walsall — To 13 Jan 02
- Vivencias: Dialogues Between the Work of Brazilian Artists 1690s–2001* — 28 Mar – 9 June 02
- Gavin Turk: Solo Show* — 27 June – 1 Sept 02
- Borders and Boundaries — 27 June – 1 Sept 02
- Works from the Collection selected by Anish Kapoor* — 19 Sept – 14 Nov 02

Warrington

Warrington Museum & Art Gallery, Bold Street, Warrington, Cheshire, WA1 1JG
tel (01925) 442392
Please phone for full details of current exhibitions.

Wells

Wells Museum, 8 Cathedral Green, Wells, Avon, BA5 2UE
tel (01749) 675337
Please phone for full details of current exhibitions.

Whitehaven

The Harbour Gallery at the Beacon, West Strand, Whitehaven, Cumbria, CA28 7LY
tel (01946) 592302
website copelandbc.gov.uk
e-mail thebeacon@copelandbc.gov.uk
The museum's collection covers the social, industrial and maritime history of Whitehaven, and includes unique Whitehaven pottery and the Beilby Goblet. The Harbour Gallery houses an annual programme of free exhibitions and events. Please phone or consult the website for full details.

Whitstable

Whitstable Museum & Gallery, 5A Oxford Street, Whitstable, Kent, CT5 1DB
tel (01227) 276998 *fax* (01227) 772379
website www.whitstable-museum.co.uk
Among the museum displays reflecting Whitstable's seafaring tradition is a notable collection of ship portraits. Events related to the collections and special exhibitions include workshops with

practising artists, for schools and colleges. Please phone or consult the website for full details of current exhibitions.

- ➤ British Gas Wildlife Photographer of the Year   26 Jan – 2 Mar 02
  Originated by the Natural History Museum, London
- ■ Whitstable Contemporary Art   9 Mar – 25 May 02
- ➤ Printers Inc: Recent British Prints   1 – 30 June 02
  NTE from the Hayward Gallery, London

Wolverhampton

Wolverhampton Art Gallery & Museum, Lichfield Street, Wolverhampton, West Midlands, WV1 1DU
tel (01902) 552055   *fax* (01902) 552053
website www.wolverhamptonart.org.uk
e-mail fineart@wag.dial.pipex.com

Wolverhampton Art Gallery and Museum holds collections of 18th-, 19th- and 20th-century painting and sculpture, including contemporary art by John Keane, Jock McFadyen, Ana Maria Pacheco, Eileen Cooper, Helen Chadwick, Lisa Milroy, Tony Bevan and others. Please phone for full details of current exhibitions.

- ■ High Summer: Photoworks by John Goto   To 9 Jan 02
- ➤ Harold Harvey: Painter of Cornwall*   To 26 Jan 02
  ➤ *Penlee House, Penzance* ➤ *Newport Museum & Art Gallery*
- ■ Sea   9 Feb – 13 Apr 02
- ■ My Generation: Contemporary Collection   Feb – Sept 02
- ■ Steve West: Mythical Echoes   27 Apr – 15 June 02
- ■ Annual Society of Artists   18 May – 28 June 02
- ■ Act it Out   29 June – 31 Aug 02
- ■ Collect and Connect: Twentyman Collection of 20th-Century Art   13 July – 14 Sept 02
- ■ Conrad Atkinson   28 Sept – 9 Nov 02

Worcester

Worcester City Museum & Art Gallery, Foregate Street, Worcester, WR1 1DT
tel (01905) 25371 *fax* (01905) 616979
Please phone for full details of current exhibitions.

Wrexham

Wrexham Arts Centre, Rhosddu Road, Wrexham, Clwyd, LL11 1AU
tel (01978) 292093 *fax* (01978) 292611
e-mail tracy.simpson@wrexham.gov.uk
Please phone for full details of current exhibitions.

- ■ Alexander Adams: Recent Paintings — 12 Jan – 23 Feb 02
- ■ Tom Giluespy* — 4 Mar – 13 Apr 02
- ■ Commonwealth — 20 Apr – 1 June 02
- ■ Terry Setch* — 8 June – 20 July
  Originated by Howard Gardens, Cardiff
- ■ Wales Drawing Biennale* — 27 July – 7 Sept 02

York

Fairfax House, Castlegate, York, YO1 9RN
tel (01904) 655543 *fax* (01904) 652262
website www.fairfaxhouse.co.uk
e-mail peterbrown@fairfaxhouse.co.uk
Please phone or consult the website for full details of current exhibitions.

York City Art Gallery, Exhibition Square, York, YO1 7EW
tel (01904) 551861 *fax* (01904) 551866
website www.york.gov.uk/heritage/museums/art
e-mail art.gallery@york.gov.uk
York City's collection reflects six hundred years of European

York (City Art Gallery)

painting, including works by Parmigianino, Bellotto, Lely, Reynolds, Frith, Boudin, Lowry and Nash, and nudes by York-born William Etty. There are also collections of watercolours, drawings and prints largely devoted to topographical views of York, and an outstanding collection of pioneer studio pottery.

- Urban: Images of Cities, Towns and Industry in Yorkshire — To 13 Jan 02
- A Brush with Nature: The Gere Collection of Landscape Studies* — 26 Jan – 7 Apr 02
  Originated by the National Gallery, London
- Justin Knowles: Sculptor — 20 Apr – 19 May 02
- Mechatronic Circus* — 27 July – 8 Sept 02
  Originated by 198 Gallery, London, and Oriel Mostyn, Llandudno
- SightSonic — 21 Sept – 3 Nov 02
- Making Journeys: Textile by Inge Hueber, Anne Keith and Veronica Togneri — 16 Nov 02 – 12 Jan 03
  Originated by Collins Gallery, Glasgow

Index

Ackroyd, Norman 59
Adams, Alexander 168
Adams, Ansel 108
Adamson, Robert 67
Ahtila, Eija Liisa 127
Ahurst, Simon 34
Aitchinson, Craigie 34
Albers, Josef 128
Allen, Colin 134
Allen, John 133
Allsop, Douglas 155
Alma-Tadema, Sir Lawrence 33, 60
Alvarez-Bravo, Manuel 129
Anderson, Blandine 36
Anderson, Michael 158
Ardizzone, Edward 38, 59, 164
Arkhipov, Vladimir 24
Arki, Junichi 148
Arnold, Eve 129
Atkinson, Conrad 167
Audubon, J. J. 94
Auerbach, Frank 44, 84, 117, 137
Austin, David 64
Ayres, Gillian 124, 137
Ayrton, Michael 14, 44, 86, 125

Backhouse, David 102
Bacon, Francis 9, 90, 139
Bala, Iwan 130
Balla, Giacomo 106
Ballard, Brian 56
Bellany, John 56
Banham, Serena 163
Banks, Claire 66
Barington, Richard Parkes 140

Barnes, Paul 66
Bass, Saul 105
Batty, Richard 164
Bayert, Ursula 29
Beardmore, S. 37
Beardsley, Aubrey 83
Beckford, William 106
Beesley, Ian 28, 79
Belcher, Heather 78
Bell, Ellen 36
Bellany, John 66, 86, 162
Bellini 22
Bellis, Kate 34
Bellotto, Bernardo 169
Bennett, Michael 45
Benton, G. 38
Bermange, Barry 25
Bernard, Joseph 86
Berry, June 98
Bersudsky, Eduard 73
Beuys, Joseph 63
Bevan, Tony 167
Beveridge, G. 48
Bewick, Thomas 59
Bik, Liesbeth 87
Black, Colin 66
Blackadder, Elizabeth 57
Blackwell, Robert 11–12
Blake, Peter 128
Bleakley, Sue 161
Bligh, Janet 160
Blondes, Jeffrey 64
Blow, Sandra 70, 151, 162
Boccioni, Umberto 106
Bomberg, David 99, 137
Bond, Marj 70
Bonnard, Pierre 9, 153

Borofsky, 165
Botticelli, Sandro 71
Boudin, Eugène 13, 169
Bourdelle, Emile Antoine 86
Brackman, David 11
Bradley, Terry 81
Brancusi, Constantine 37
Breton, Jules 55
Breughel 101
Bridge, Eoghan 34, 36
Briggs, David 162, 163
Brimage, Esther 51
Broadbent, Stephen 102
Brook, Peter 79
Brow, Mary 66
Brown, John 66
Brown, Peter 17
Brown, Trevor 81
Bucher, Mayo 30
Buckle, Janet 51
Buckler, S. 37
Burne-Jones, Sir Edward Coley 32, 33, 94, 137
Burns, Brendan 138
Burns, Glynnis 51
Burra, Edward 33
Bushe, Chris 66
Buxton, Albert Sorby 133
Byrne, John 73

Calderon, Philip Hermogenes 30
Cameron, D. Y. 145
Canaletto 13, 37, 105, 152
Card, 165

Index

Caro, Anthony 67, 100
Carpenter, Pip 36
Carrà, Carlo 106
Carracci 142
Carrick, Ian 102
Carrington, Sarah 66
Carter, David 36
Caulfield, Patrick 44, 128, 164
Cézanne, Paul 37, 39, 120
Chadwick, Helen 167
Chadwick, Lynn 14, 99, 117–18
Chagall, Marc 34, 163
Chalayan, Hussein 151
Chalmers, George Paul 71
Chamberlain, Brenda 134
Chandrika 28
Chapman, John L. 25
Chardin, Jean Baptiste Siméon 17, 73
Chessin, Laura 32
Chirico, Giorgio de 106
Clarke, Jonathan 34
Clarke, Stuart 47
Claude Lorraine 11, 105
Clements, Eric 23
Coates, Andrew 19
Coker, Charles 77
Coles, Howard 60
Colvin, Calum 67
Conroy, Stephen 118
Constable, John 33, 37, 64, 83, 95, 120, 124
Cook, Ian 63
Cooke, Barrie 53
Cooper, Eileen 167
Cooper, Samuel 153
Cooper, Susie 159
Cornish, Charlotte 34, 36
Cotman, John Snell 84

Cotter, Maud 56
Couch, Christopher 118
Cowen, William 149
Cox, David 33
Cox, Philip 133
Cranston, Andrew 154
Crook, P.J. 76
Cross, Dorothy 53, 84
Cunliffe, Peter 25
Cunningham, Paul 51
Cunningham, William 81
Curnow-Vosper, Sydney 134
Currie, John 159
Currie, Ken 40
Cutts, Susan 158
Cuyp, Aelbert 120

Dali, Salvador 67
Dalou, Jules-Aimée 86
Darragh, Ian 51
Daulton, Keith 136
Daulton, Sue 136
Davey, 165
Davidson, Colin 12, 56
Davidson, Jenny 81
Davie, Alan 57, 73, 159
Davies, John 129, 139
Davies, Marcelle 29
Davies, Ogwyn 161
Davis, Emma 162
Day, Patricia McKinnon 134
Deakin, John 129
Degas, Edgar 37, 165
Delacroix, Eugène 165
Depres, Ravi 139
Dicksee, Frank 90
Dimitrijevic, Braco 22, 24
Dobrowolski, Chris 85
Doherty, Willie 53
Donald, George 65
Donaldson, Emma 50
Donovan, James 138

Donovan, Terence 68, 153
Dove, Stanley 34, 36
Dowe, Virginia 36
Draper, Matthew 66
Dubuffet, Jean 87, 110, 128
Duncan, Ana 56
Duncan, Jean 20
Dupont, Gainsborough 160
Dyce, William 90

Eardley, Joan 57, 145
Eaves, John 11
Edwards, Deborah 66
Edwards, Jilly 57
Egan, Felim 53, 64
Egerton, Dumas 67
Elias, Ken 46
Epstein, Jacob 38, 83, 94, 99, 165
Ernst, Max 67
Essen, Lizanne van 156
Etty, William 169
Eun-Mo, Chung 53
Everett, John 80
Eyck, Jan van 119

Fell, Sheila 45
Ferguson, Chris J. 57
Fergusson, J.D. 144
Finlay, Ian Hamilton 64, 151
Fitzgerald, Patrick M. 56
Flanagan, Barry 128
Fleck, Conor 51
Flynn, Liam 66
Foley, John 94
Foreman, William 102
Francis, Mark 53
Freud, Lucian 17, 84, 94, 126
Frew, Iuan 51
Frickers, Gordon 11

171

Index

Friedel, Su Kyung Yu 34
Frink, Elisabeth 14, 32, 34, 94, 165
Frith, William Powell 169
Frost, Anthony 162
Frost, Terry 15, 34, 159, 161
Fulton, Hamish 126
Furness, T. 48

Gadd, Gerald 148
Gainsborough, Thomas 15, 22, 32, 37, 38, 76, 83, 92, 105, 112, 120, 126, 152, 159
Gal, Hannah 32
Gales, Simon 102
Galliano, John 105
Gates-McQuaid, Fiona 41
Gaubo, Naum 151
Gaudier-Brzeska, 37, 83
Géricault, Theodore 165
Gertler, Mark 99
Giacometti, Alberto 139
Gilbert, Mark 69, 87, 121
Gill, Eric 83, 163
Gillespie, Rowan 56
Gillespie, Sarah 146
Gillies, William George 67
Gillray, James 164
Gilman, Harold 155
Giluespy, Tom 168
Godbold, David 53
Goldin, Nan 129
Goldsworthy, Andy 64
Gordon, Douglas 108
Gormley, Antony 40, 101, 108
Gosling, Joyce 41

Goto, John 167
Goya, Francisco 13, 97, 110, 120
Graham, Rigby 164
Gravelot, Hubert-François 160
Greco, El 11, 13, 64
Grevatte, Jenny 70
Griffiths, Diane 136
Grimshaw, Atkinson 30
Groener, Anita 56
Grosse, Katharina 24
Guardi, Francesco 15, 152
Gussin, Graham 24

Hale, Jennie 66
Hals, Franz 37, 112, 142
Hambling, Maggi 118, 161
Hamilton, Ann 52
Hamilton, Ken 51
Hamilton, Pamela 81
Hamilton, Richard 24, 53
Hamnett, Nina 162
Hampson, Frank 69
Hanlon, Maire 56
Harding, Alexis 56
Harrigan, Claire 66
Harris, George Frederick 134
Harris, Sue Hiley 29
Hartley, Ben 17
Harvey, Harold 167
Hayman, Francis 160
Hayter, Stanley William 125
Henderson, Nigel 63, 153
Hepworth, Barbara 15, 37, 44, 67, 150, 159, 164, 165
Herald, James Waterson 71

Heron, Patrick 159
Herring, J. F. 30
Hicks, Nicola 17, 30
Hicks-Jenkins, Clive 29
Higgins, Leo 56
Hill, David Octavius 67
Hill, Derek 20
Hill, D.O. 145
Hill, Paul 50
Hillerby, Claire 66
Hilton, Wil 41
Hirst, Damien 63
Hitchens, Ivor 161
Hobbema, Meindert 105
Hockney, David 95, 109, 125, 138
Hodgkin, Howard 64, 96, 161
Hodgkins, Frances 60
Hogarth, William 9, 37, 90, 105
Holbein, Hans 11, 153
Holland, Derek 146
Holloway, Edgar 29, 98
Hones, Aneurin 46
Horrabin, J. F. 103
House, Lisa 48
House, Michelle 78
Howson, Peter 162
Hoyland, John 34, 162
Hudson, Thomas 32
Hueber, Inge 73, 169
Huebler, Douglas 102
Hughes, David Gordon 12
Hunt, Holman 137
Huygue, Pierre 111
Hyslop, Alisia 36

Innes, Calum 64
Innocent, Liz 41
Ipchilz 104
Irvin, Albert 34

Jack, Hillary 157

Index

Jacklin, Don 51
Jackson, Kurt 45, 69, 162, 163
James, Alfred 134
James, Jeremy 66
Jeffreys, Rachael 162
John, Augustus 39, 83, 94, 130, 161, 162
John, Gwen 39, 161, 162
Johnson, John 46
Johnson, Tim 138
Johnston, John 41
Jones, David 37
Jones, Mary Lloyd 130
Jones, Ruth 50
Jordan, Eithne 56
Joseph, Jane 17
Judd, Donald 99–100, 127
Judge-Furstova, Mila 24

Kalvis, Claire 66
Kandinsky, Wassily 90
Kane, Michael 56
Kauffmann, Angelica 146
Keane, John 167
Keeley, Laura 68
Keith, Anne 73, 169
Kelland, Andrea 160
Kelly, Percy 45
Kenna, Michael 129
Kerr, Tom 51
King, 165
Kingston, Angela Hoppe 160
Kinney, Desmond 56
Kirchner, Ernst Ludwig 67
Kitaj, R. B. 118, 120, 137
Klee, Paul 108
Klein, Anita 34
Kneller, Godfrey 152

Knight, Laura 38, 145
Knowles, Emma 46
Knowles, Justin 169
Knowles, Mike 46
Kokoschka, Oscar 118
Kollwitz, Käthe 110
König, Heidi 103
Koninck, Philips de 73
Kossoff, Leon 104
Kramer, 99
Kuen-Shan, Kwong 29
Kunisada 22

La Dell, Edwin 149
La Thangue, H. H. 149
Lamb, Lynton 41
Lancaster, W. 48
Landseer, Sir Edwin 33, 137
Lanyon, Peter 100
Large, Catherine 32
Laroon, Marcellus 146
Larusdottir, Karolina 34, 36
Laurence, Thomas 145
Lavery, Sir John 84
Law, Deborah 68
Lawrence, Sir Thomas 97
Lawson, Sonia 70
Le Brun, Christopher 161
Lear, Edward 32, 84
Lees, Michael 11
Leighton, Lord Frederic 94
Lely, Sir Peter 105, 153, 169
Lenkiewicz, Robert 146
Leonardo da Vinci 11, 92, 142, 153
Lewitt, Sol 52, 165
Linnell, John 33
Lloyd-Griffith, David 46
Long, Richard 32, 69, 151

Lord, Sally Greaves 78
Loten, David 46
Loveday, Ross 36
Lowry, L. S. 33, 86, 90, 149, 156, 158, 169
Lucas, Samuel 81
Lyons, Mike 133

McAllister, Therese 56
McCall, Susan 33
McCarthy, Paul 94
McCartney, Paul 95
McClary, Louise 146, 162
McCullin, Don 69
McCulloch, Horatio 145
MacDonald, Hamish 162
MacDonald, Margaret 71
MacDonald, Melville 71
MacDonald, Patricia 64
McDonnell, Hector 56
McEwan, Angus 65
McFadyen, Jock 167
MacInnes, Jock 66
McIntosh, Archie Dunbar 66
McKeever, Ian 96
McKendrick, Tom 73
McKenna, Rollie 38
MacKenna, Stephen 53
Mackeown, James 19
Mackie, Christina 88
Mackinnon-Day, Patricia 133
Mackintosh, Charles Rennie 67, 73, 106
McKittrick, Amanda 20
McLaughlin, Tricia 48
McLean, John 64
Maclean, Mary 73
Maclellan, Donald 67
McMurray, Katty 103
McTaggart, John Maxwell 57

Index

McTaggart, William 67, 86, 145
McWhirter, Isabel 46
Madriz, Carlos 122
Magill, Elizabeth 53
Magritte, René 22, 67
Maguire, Brian 53
Maillol, Aristide 86
Malone, Jim 45
Manet, Édouard 142
Marc, Franz 90
Marr, Jacqueline 60
Marshall, David 41
Marshman, Tom 32
Martin, David 65
Martin, Kenneth 82, 109
Martin, Malcolm 66
Martin, Mary 146
Martini, Simone 36
Mason, Gareth 158
Matisse, Henri 21, 34, 67, 96, 110, 127, 128, 153
Mawudokiu, Derek 119
Mayes, Emerson 79
Mellis, Margaret 159
Melville, Derek 81
Meninsky, 99
Metcalfe, Muriel 164
Michelangelo Buonarroti 11, 142
Millais, J. E. 58, 124, 145
Miller, Garry Fabian 153
Mills, Eleri 130
Mills, Ernestine 18
Mills, Jon 30
Milroy, Lisa 96, 161, 167
Miró, Joan 96, 128
Modigliani, Amedeo 106
Monet, Claude 9, 22, 37, 53, 64, 120, 165

Monkhouse, Charles 34, 149
Moon, Jeremy 153
Moon, Mick 96
Moore, Henry 38, 44, 60, 67, 83, 86, 99, 128, 135, 138, 139, 156, 164
Moores, John 95
Morandi, Giorgio 106, 128
Moray, Shara 156
Morgan, Edwin 67
Morgan, Jenny 11
Morgan, Tina 18
Morris, John Meirion 46
Morris, Mali 139
Morris, Sir Cedric 134
Morrison, Paul 155
Morrocco, Alberto 66
Muñoz, Juan 127
Murillo, Bartholomé 105
Murray-Orr, Craig 64
Muspratt, Helen 79
Myers, Mark 11
Mytens, Lawrance 152

Nash, Paul 9, 44, 138, 153, 165, 169
Naughton, James 79
Neave, Vincent 11
Nevitt, Diane 146
Newman, Barnett 127
Newman, Hayley 24
Newson, Marc 105
Nicholson, Ben 9, 32, 37, 44, 83, 84, 100, 159
Nicholson, Sarah 158
Nicholson, William 60
Nicholson, Winifred 37, 40
Noble, Lewis 34, 49
Noon, Aaronson 36
Norris, Charles 162
Nreakey, John 19

Oakley, Charles 45
Oliver, Isaac 153
O'Malley, Tony 84, 146
Opie, Julian 96
O'Reilly, Philip 28

Pacheco, Ana Maria 167
Padhilla, Eduardo 122
Pane, Gina 155
Paolozzi, Eduard 63
Pareno, Phillipa 111
Parkinson, Mark 158
Parmigianino 169
Parr, Martin 98
Parrott, Helen 163
Parsons, Vicken 151
Pasmore, Victor 33, 118, 125
Paterson, J. 48
Paul, Darren 51
Pearce, Bryan 15, 146
Peascod, Bill 45
Peploe, S. J. 86
Perring, Susie 36
Perry, Grayson 158
Pether, Henry 77
Pettigrew, Jennifer 66
Philipson, 67
Phipps, Howard 17, 44
Picasso, Pablo 34, 37, 44, 67, 69, 77, 96, 110, 111, 125, 127, 128, 165
Pien, Ed 134
Piero Della Francesca 119
Piper, John 14, 34, 164
Piranesi, Giovanni Battista 39
Pisanello, 120
Pissarro, 9, 83
Plumptre, William 45
Pol, Jos van der 87
Potter, Beatrix 145

Index

Poussin, Nicolas 11, 22, 105, 111
Powell, William 90
Power, Mark 129
Pretsele, Philomaena 150
Price, Trevor 36
Prior, Cath 158
Procter, R. 34
Prosser, Henry 77
Provan, Donald 65
Pugh, Tim 148
Puvis de Chavannes 22

Rae, Barbara 45, 57, 162
Raeburn, Sir Henry 9
Rainey, Lesley 81
Ramsay, Allan 73
Raphael 11, 142
Raphael, Sarah 118
Ratcliffe, William 155
Rauschenberg, Robert 100
Ravilious, Eric 60
Ravilious, James 162
Redpath, Anne 67, 86, 145
Rego, Paula 118
Reilly, Angela 63
Rembrandt 64, 71, 73, 95, 101, 105, 112, 120
Renoir, Pierre-Auguste 22, 37, 39, 53, 120
Reynolds, Sir Joshua 9, 32, 73, 105, 112, 124, 137, 146, 152, 169
Rhys, Shani 130
Rice, Brian 147
Richards, Ceri 39, 44
Richardson, Matthew 29
Richardson, Ray 34
Richardson, Victor 56

Riley, Bridget 75, 84, 85, 109
Roberts, Will 46
Robertson, Grace 30
Roche, François 111
Rodin, Auguste 39, 86
Romney, George 84, 95, 121, 149
Roper, Geoff 61
Rossetti, Dante Gabriel 22, 58
Rossi, Carlo 162
Rouault, Georges 23
Rowney, George 13
Rubens, Peter Paul 11, 22, 37, 65, 97, 105, 140, 152
Ruff, Thomas 52
Ruscha, Ed 142
Ruskin, John 84
Russell, John 77
Russolo, Luigi 106
Ruysdael, Salomon van 146
Rysbrack, John Michael 32

Sage, Henry 77
Sainsbury, Jonathon 12
Savage, Jenny 149
Schleger, Hans 117
Schnyder, Jean Frederic 24
Schober, 33
Schofield, David 66
Schwitters, Kurt 84, 136
Scott, Patrick 84
Scott, William 15
Scouller, Glen 66, 163
Scully, Kate 149
Scully, Sean 64
See-Paynton, Colin 17, 46
Serra, Richard 165
Setch, Terry 72, 168

Seurat, Georges 120
Severini, Gino 106
Shanahan, Séan 53
Shapiro, 165
Sharma, Rakhee 60
Sharp, Nelina 156
Shepherd, E. H. 42, 78
Shiomi, Nana 24
Shoji, Satoru 30
Shore, Jack 46
Shotton, M. 48
Shrigley, David 102
Sickert, Walter 32, 44, 83, 86, 138, 158, 161
Sidén, Ann-Sofi 108
Sierra, Santiago 24
Signer, Roman 102
Sisley, Alfred 9
Slater, Richard 12
Slattery, Nicola 36
Sloan, Hamilton 51
Smith, Rita 48
Smith, Ronald 162
Smoothey, Ronald 77
Smythe, Helen 65
Snow, Michel 155
Sonnabend, Paul 17
Spackman, Sarah 56
Spence, Annora 103
Spencer, Stanley 21, 46, 83, 84, 90, 124, 137, 149, 153
Srivastava, Durgesh 25
Stanfield, Clarkson 33
Stanton, L. 37
Starling, Simon 151
Steele-Perkins, Chris 25, 160
Steer, Philip Wilson 83
Stefano, Arturo di 82
Stirling, Dorothy 34
Stone, Marcus 30
Stork, Mary 146
Stuart, Imogen 56
Stubbs, George 15, 73

175

Index

Suschitzky, Wolfgang 67
Sutherland, Graham 44, 47, 100, 118, 125, 138, 164

Tàpies, Antoni 128
Taplin, Guy 17
Taylor, E. A. 57
Teniers, David 97, 105
Tenniel, John 59
Terbrugghen, Hendrik 53
Testino, Mario 121
Thackeray, Janet 81
Thimothy, Annie 43
Thompson, Jacob 81
Thompson, Suzann 28
Thompson, Tim 11
Thorpe, Hilary 138
Thursfield, R. 37
Tiepolo, Giovanni 13, 105
Tilson, Joe 96
Tinsley, Joanna 81
Tintoretto 142
Tissot, James 18, 38
Titchell, John 38
Titian 11, 36, 104
Togneri, Veronica 73, 169
Tovey, David 163
Towell, Larry 103
Tremlett, David 150
Tress, David 70
Trickett, Mike 60
Tucker, William 165
Tuff, Richard 103
Turk, Gavin 165
Turner, J. M. W. 15, 33, 64, 76, 84, 92, 94, 95, 112, 120, 124

Uglow, Geoff 61, 63
Umaña-Clarke 103
Unsworth, Luke 24

Uzmen, Aytac 41

Van Dyck, Anthony 11, 22, 37, 55, 104, 105, 112, 152
Van Gogh, Vincent 64, 120, 165
Vaughan, Justin 81
Vaux, Marc 100
Vayreda, C. 102
Velazquez, Diego da Silva y 64, 97, 120
Velde, van de 146
Venables, David 51
Veneziano, 36
Vermeer, Jan 64, 112, 120
Veronese, Paolo 37, 142
Vuillard, Édouard 67

Waal, Edmund de 154
Wagh, Iberhim 156
Walch, Ken 43
Walke, Ethel 149
Walker, Jason 162
Walker, Michele 30
Wallinger, Mark 129, 158
Wallis, Alfred 159
Walpole, Lon 78
Walsh, Samuel 56
Ward, John 38, 69
Warhol, Andy 125, 127
Warner, Paul 146
Waterhouse, John William 33
Waters, Alan 158
Watson, B. 48
Watson, Paul 51
Watt, Alison 64, 73
Watt, Jackie 66
Watteau, Jean-Antoine 105
Webb, Boyd 106

Weight, Carel 38
Weightman, Alison 65
Welsh, Robin 34
Wentworth, 165
Wesson, Edward 77
West, Steve 167
Weston, Edward 110
Whatmore, Nel 79
Whistler, James McNeill 71, 73, 106
White, Barry 158
White, David 66
Wilkie, David 97, 106
Williams, Catrin 130
Williams, Emrys 138
Williams, Glynn 100
Williams, Ian 148
Williams, Kyffin 130, 134
Williams, Penry 134
Willoughby, Chris 162
Wilson, Edward 42
Wilson, James Glen 20
Wilson, Richard 39, 154
Wilson, Tony 31
Wint, Peter de 91
Wither, Kirsty 65
Wlérick, Robert 86
Wood, Christopher 37
Wood, Craig 95
Wood, Michael Brennand 78
Wood, Silas 24
Wormell, Chris 17
Wright, Joseph 94
Wright, Peter 138

Yass, Catherine 96, 137
Yates, Fred 146
Yeats, Jack 134
Young, Carey 139
Young, Emily 64

Zhongsen, Chen 56